Radical Lutherans/
Lutheran Radicals

Radical Lutherans/
Lutheran Radicals

EDITED BY

Jason A. Mahn

CASCADE *Books* · Eugene, Oregon

RADICAL LUTHERANS / LUTHERAN RADICALS

Cascade Books
An Imprint of Wipf and Stock Publishers
199 W. 8th Ave., Suite 3
Eugene, OR 97401

www.wipfandstock.com

PAPERBACK ISBN: 978-1-4982-3491-7
HARDCOVER ISBN: 978-1-4982-3493-1
EBOOK ISBN: 978-1-4982-3492-4

Cataloging-in-Publication data:

Names: Mahn, Jason A., editor.

Title: Radical Lutherans / Lutheran radicals / edited by Jason A. Mahn.

Description: Eugene, OR: Cascade Books | Includes bibliographical references.

Identifiers: ISBN: 978-1-4982-3491-7 (PAPERBACK) | ISBN: 978-1-4982-3493-1 (HARDCOVER) | ISBN: 978-1-4982-3492-4 (EBOOK).

Subjects: Lutheran church—Doctrines | Luther, Martin, 1483–1546 | Kierkegaard, Søren, 1813–1855 | Bonhoeffer, Dietrich, 1906–1945 | Sölle, Dorothee.

Classification: BR315 R31 2017 (print) | BR315 (ebook).

Manufactured in the U.S.A.

"For you are powerful not that you may make the weak weaker by oppression, but that you may make them powerful by raising them up and defending them."

—MARTIN LUTHER, "TWO KINDS OF RIGHTEOUSNESS"

Contents

Contributors

Jacqueline Bussie is Professor of Religion and Director of the Forum on Faith and Life at Concordia College, Moorhead, Minnesota. Her first book, *The Laughter of the Oppressed: Ethical and Theological Resistance in Wiesel, Morrison, and Endo* (Bloomsbury T&T Clark, 2007), won the national Trinity Prize. Her latest book, *Outlaw Christian: Finding Authentic Faith by Breaking the "Rules"* (Thomas Nelson/HarperCollins 2016), provides ways to handle difficult and troubling questions of life. Through interfaith understanding initiatives and other means, Bussie and Concordia students work to make the world a more compassionate place.

Lori Brandt Hale is Associate Professor of Religion at Augsburg College in Minneapolis, Minnesota. She is an international scholar of Dietrich Bonhoeffer, Secretary for the International Bonhoeffer Society (English Language Section), and co-author of *Bonhoeffer for Armchair Theologians* (Westminster John Knox, 2009), which introduces Bonhoeffer to nonspecialized audiences. In her teaching, Hale challenges students to recognize that their philosophical and existential questions (Who am I? Why am I here?) might just have theological answers.

Carl S. Hughes is Assistant Professor of Theology at Texas Lutheran University in Seguin, Texas. He is the author of *Kierkegaard and the Staging of Desire: Rhetoric and Performance in a Theology of Eros* (Fordham University Press, 2014) and the Secretary-Treasurer of the Søren Kierkegaard Society (USA). His interests include the theology of the cross; the intersections of theology, race, and gender; the possibilities of biblical interpretation; and theological responses to religious pluralism. Some of his favorite courses to teach at TLU are Critics and Defenders of Faith in the Modern Age; Life and Writings of Martin Luther; and Theologies of the Civil Rights Movement.

Jason A. Mahn is Associate Professor of Religion and Director of the Presidential Center for Faith and Learning at Augustana College, Rock Island, Illinois. He is the author of *Fortunate Fallibility: Kierkegaard and the Power of Sin* (Oxford University Press, 2011) and *Becoming a Christian in Christendom: Radical Discipleship and the Way of the Cross in America's "Christian" Culture* (Fortress, 2016), as well as editor of *The Vocation of Lutheran Higher Education* (Lutheran University Press, 2016). Mahn's favorite courses to teach at Augustana include Suffering, Death, and Endurance; Luther: Life, Thought, and Legacy; and a course taught in Holden Village, Creator, Creation, and Calling.

Samuel Torvend is Professor of the History of Christianity and holds the endowed University Chair in Lutheran Studies at Pacific Lutheran University in Tacoma, Washington, where he teaches courses on Luther, the Lutheran Heritage, Lutheran Political Commitments, and Women Reformers. He is the author of *Luther and The Hungry Poor: Gathered Fragments* (Fortress, 2008; Wipf & Stock, 2017); *Flowing Water, Uncommon Birth: Christian Baptism in a Post-Christian Culture* (Augsburg, 2011); and *Daily Bread, Holy Meal: Opening the Gifts of Holy Communion* (Augsburg, 2004). Since 2012, Torvend has worked closely with Radicalizing Reformation, an international network of academics promoting social justice, peace-making, and reconciliation through scholarship and activism.

Abbreviations

Works by Martin Luther

LW   Luther, Martin. *Luther's Works.* American Edition. 55 vols. Edited by Jaroslav Pelikan and Helmut T. Lehman. Philadelphia: Muehlenberg and Fortress, and St. Louis: Concordia, 1955–86
(Title of the work will be followed by the abbreviation LW, and then volume number, colon [:], and page number.)

BTW   Luther, Martin. *Martin Luther's Basic Theological Writings.* 2nd ed. Edited by Timothy F. Lull. Minneapolis: Fortress, 2005
(Title of the work will be followed by the abbreviation *BTW* and then page number.)

Works by Søren Kierkegaard

JP   *Søren Kierkegaard's Journals and Papers.* Edited and translated by Howard V. Hong and Edna H. Hong, assisted by Gregor Malantschuk. 7 vols. Bloomington: Indiana University Press, 1967–1978
(The abbreviation *JP* will be followed by volume number, colon [:], entry number, date in parenthesis, and finally page number marked by "p.")

KW   *Kierkegaard's Writings.* Edited and translated by Howard V. Hong and Edna H. Hong. 26 vols. Princeton: Princeton University Press, 1978–2002

(Shortened title of the work will be followed by the abbreviation KW, and then volume number, colon [:], and
page number.)

Works by Dietrich Bonhoeffer

DBWE *Dietrich Bonhoeffer Works.* English Edition. Edited by
Wayne Whitson Floyd Jr., et al. 17 vols. Minneapolis:
Fortress, 1996–present
(Title of the work will be followed by the abbreviation
DBWE, and then volume number, colon [:], and page
number.)

All quotations from the Bible are from the New Revised Standard Version.

Introduction

Jason A. Mahn

If you closed your eyes and meditated on the word *Lutheran*, what would you imagine?

Many might hear the voice of Garrison Keillor, original host of the radio variety show, *A Prairie Home Companion*, whose fictitious Lake Wobegon is set in the center of Midwestern Lutheran country. Some might smell church-basement green-bean-and-tater-tot-hotdish or picture fruit-filled Jello with marshmallows on top; others will think of 95 theses posted to the door of a sixteenth-century German church. If you have ever attended a Lutheran Church (it probably had a red front door) or went to a Lutheran College (many with a required course in religion), you might associate the word with "justification by grace through faith." (For emphasis, some will add: "apart from the works of the law.") You might even recall some additional details about Martin Luther's place in the Protestant Reformation— or in the Church's *schism*, as a faithful Catholic might put it. Some might even think about their own *vocations*—a word that describes the Lutheran understanding that daily tasks and responsibilities serve God whenever and wherever they serve a neighbor in need.

Now think of the word *radical*.

Do any of the same images come to mind? Garrison Keillor wearing a red beret? Quilting groups raising their fists against "the man"? Probably not.

Can Lutherans or Lutheranism as a whole be radical? If so, in what ways? Lutherans and others from mainline (and mainstream) denominations won't seem obviously "radical" to many Generation Xers—those who grew up in the wake of the 1960s' counterculture, with its sexual liberation, feminist manifestos, drug experimentation, grassroots political protests, and other more noticeably radical revolutions. Millennials, those emerging adults and multitasking pragmatists in their teens and 20s, might be

1

unconcerned with the whole issue. They are too busy competing to get into selective colleges or scrounging for ways to pay for them; for them, church and other inherited institutions seem only to detract from authentic living. Indeed, for many if not most of us, *radical* and *Lutheran* are words only strangely juxtaposed. Isn't Lutheranism all-too mainstream, normal, and nice? Isn't it something of the default or customary religion of the Midwest, which is itself so very mundane—"flyover" country for hipper coastal urbanites? What's so radical about Minnesota accents (doh-nt-cha noh)? Or about the *Lutheran Book of Worship* (*LBW*), bobbleheads of a plump reformer, or the "free grace" that ostensibly tells each of us that we're pretty good the way that we are?

The five authors of this book collectively make the case that *Lutherans* who fight for *radical* political, cultural, and economic reforms, as well as *radicals* who are theologically, denominationally, and faithfully *Lutheran*, comprise an important stand of the intellectual and ecclesial (church) tradition called Lutheran and that the words and witnesses by these radical Lutherans/Lutheran radicals ought to be taken seriously.

The penetrating theologies and sometimes extreme socio-political undertakings of such radicals might surprise or even startle many of us in North America. After all, we live in a dominant culture where *Lutheran*, *Christian*, and especially *church* seem ever so normal and normative. Many leave church for exactly that reason. A recent survey by the Pew Foundation finds the number of the nonaffiliated (those not affiliating with any religion) or "nones" (those who check "none" when asked about their religion on a questionnaire) to be increasing quite dramatically—up from 16.1 percent in 2007 to 22.8 percent in 2014. There are 56 million religiously unaffiliated adults in the United States today. "Nones" include not only self-described atheists and agnostics (7 percent in 2014, up from 4 percent in 2007), but also those who do not embrace these terms, but still describe their own religious outlook as "nothing in particular." The religiously unaffiliated are more numerous than either Catholics or all mainline Protestants (Lutherans included) grouped together; among religious groups, they are now second in numbers only to evangelical Protestants.[1]

The religiously unaffiliated are some of the sharpest critics of what they perceive as support for the status quo by organized religions. People in this group are much more likely than the general public "to say that churches and other religious organizations are too concerned with money

---

1. "America's Changing Religious Landscape." See also Lipka, "A Closer Look."

and power, too focused on rules, and too involved in politics." And yet, curiously, a solid majority of the unaffiliated continues to think that religion is good for society, with 78 percent saying religious organizations bring people together and help strengthen community bonds, and 77 percent saying religious organizations play an important role in aiding the disenfranchised.[2]

These numbers suggest that more and more people in the United States—especially Millennials and younger adults[3]—harbor a good deal of ambivalence with regards to church.[4] They appreciate the community-aspect of religious institutions and the good that they do for the poor and marginalized; still, they perceive churches as having an all-too-cozy relationship with dominant culture, traditional values, and everything considered conventional. In other words, church seems all too mainstream, and many either feel marginalized by it or—more commonly—assume that any edginess or authenticity would be difficult to find there.

We tend to forget that the Lutheran reform movement was more than the start of a new branch of the church catholic (in fact, Martin Luther and his fellow reformers never wanted that). The "evangelical" or, later, "Lutheran" reform movement in sixteenth-century Europe also initiated the first food assistance programs for the hungry, health care for the vulnerable, housing for orphans, public education for both boys and girls, and other massive socio-political reforms.[5] If such assistance seems common now, it is because early Christian reformers normalized this care for the needy precisely when it was not considered normal. Today, the Evangelical Lutheran Church in America (ELCA) tirelessly pursues social transformation, with flagship disaster response teams, immigration and refugee services, and other social ministry organizations. What is more, such initiatives—then and now—spring directly from what Lutheran Christians consider the center of their faith: God's unmerited acceptance of sinful human beings.

2. "'Nones' on the Rise."

3. The unaffiliated are a diverse group; still, they are on average quite a bit younger than churchgoers and others who call themselves Christian. The median age of unaffiliated adults is 36; compare this to the general adult population's median age (46), the median age of mainline Protestant (52), and the median age of Catholics (49). "America's Changing Religious Landscape."

4. Avoiding both definitive belief and resolute disbelief, they may in fact hover in the margins with an "ironist's faith." See Taylor, *Varieties of Religion Today*, 56–60.

5. See chapter 1, where Samuel Torvend highlights just how central such social and economic reforms were to Luther and the Lutheran reform movement.

Having been freed from interminable attempts to please God, people can finally recognize and respond to the needs of other creatures, especially to the needs of the seemingly godforsaken.

Rightly construed and properly mobilized, *radical Lutherans* (i.e. those who want to get back to the core of their theological tradition) ineluctably become *Lutheran radicals*: those freed by God's gracious word to engage in social and political reforms that are often subversive of "the way things are." While the authors of this book think both senses of *radical* can and should come together, there are some who want to reform the church and its theology (literally, its way of thinking about God) while remaining ambivalent, if not suspicious, of Christians who take to the streets.

One example comes from some thirty years ago, when the Commission for a New Lutheran Church conducted a study of whether and how various Lutheran church bodies might be combined into one Lutheran church in America. After the committee members completed their work and as the new Evangelical Lutheran Church in America was being unveiled, Gerhard Forde, the best known theologian at the largest Lutheran seminary in the United States, penned a temperature-taking first essay for the inaugural issue of *Lutheran Quarterly*. Entitling the essay, "Radical Lutheranism," Forde traced the recently mainline, increasingly mainstream, and (for him) thoroughly accommodated identity of Lutheranism to the loss of its theological center. According to Forde, Lutherans were wanting to moderate Martin Luther's unambiguous proclamation of grace alone (only God saves!) with a more optimistic anthropology (humans might contribute something, too) and so much talk about social transformation. American Lutherans were thus forfeiting their reason for being. In his words, "Virtually all the failures and shortcomings of Lutheranism can be seen in the hesitancy to proclaim the gospel in uncompromising, unconditional fashion, to proclaim as though we were about the business of summoning the dead to life, calling new beings into existence."[6] From this sentence—and so many others that Forde crafted—it is clear that for him "radical Lutheranism" means Lutheranism returned to its central *churchly* mission, namely, to administer the sacraments and preach the power of an unqualified Gospel.

The ostensible blandness of Lutheranism in North America today might simply confirm Forde's fears in retrospect. Perhaps today's ELCA, with its ten million members, ten thousand congregations, and twenty-six

6. Forde, "Radical Lutheranism," 13.

colleges and universities, looks and feels more and more mainline and mainstream. Sit through any given ELCA service and it might seem Catholic in its liturgy, evangelical in its piety, humanistic in its theology, or simply church-like in its donuts and coffee. For many, *Lutheran*—beside *Methodist, Episcopalian, Baptist, Presbyterian, Catholic,* and even *emergent* or *nondenominational*—seems to denote slightly different packaging covering a fairly homogenized product, like one more version of Cheerios crowding the cereal aisle shelves. Does this mean that the "America" in "Evangelical Lutheran Church in America" has become more determinative for Lutheran beliefs and practices than its identity as a Reformation church, as gathered around the *Evangelion* or Good News? Certainly, too, the ELCA does pursue social transformation, with those aforementioned disaster response teams, immigration support services, and programs to resettle refugees. Does this prove Forde's concern that it is losing its theological center, swapping justification by grace through faith for belief that we mere humans might save ourselves?

Radically Lutheran *and* Lutheranly Radical

The authors of this book think that Lutheran churches, colleges, and individuals can be radical, and even *more* radical—or *differently* radical—than Forde imagines. Forde wanted to radicalize Lutherans in the original, etymological sense of the word. From *radix,* or the *root* of a thing, to be *radical* means to attend to one's foundation or essence—to be deeply grounded in the soil from which one comes. Accordingly, Lutherans should return to their Reformation roots, perhaps to a time before Lutheranism landed on American soil and became what might look like just another denomination. Such re-rooting would entail the unconditional confession of grace alone, an utter trust in the life-giving power of the sacraments, and the courage to preach and hear God's good news, unleashing its power to crush self-serving ambitions while resurrecting new life and hope through Jesus. This *is* radical stuff, especially in twenty-first-century America, with its penchant for self-reliance, and notwithstanding the facile association of "radical" with flowerchildren in the 60s or anti-institutionalism (including "anti-churchism") today. In fact, all of the college professors authoring this book also preach "Good News" or otherwise try to name the roots of ultimate hope and new life. We understand that being *professors* sometimes entails *professing* the faith that is within us or that we see in our students.

But perhaps because our primary work is within Lutheran higher education rather than Lutheran congregations, we do not understand Lutheranism to be *contained* within churches and their performative proclamations. We think that the Lutheran tradition has other roots that are just as deep as the proclamation of the Gospel but branch out beyond the ministry of Word and Sacrament. Might Lutheranism be radical in the socio-political sense as well? Could it be a force for tremendous social liberation, a movement that seeks, serves, and remains in solidarity with the most vulnerable and marginalized in society today: the poor and suffering, those out-casted, vilified, forgotten, and scapegoated? Might you find the most radical Lutherans not only in pulpits and pews but also in classrooms, not to mention the streets, in labor rights movements, international peace teams, prisons, and poorhouses? Beyond confessional and denominational Lutheranism, there is a distinctive theo-political tradition composed of people who have been shaped by Martin Luther the theological thinker and political protestor.

What is more, the authors of this book believe that being theologically or ecclesially radical (deeply rooted in the Lutheran tradition) and participating in grassroots movements for social justice (radical politics) *at best go hand in hand*. We live, of course, in a dominant culture where traditional Christianity and progressivist politics seem to pull in opposite directions. Our culture also tends to assume that, if you are faithful to a religious community, you ought not criticize it—at least not deeply. Yet Lutherans at their best *both* conserve orthodox understandings of God's grace and forgiveness *and* work to extend and even radicalize that grace by acting in solidarity with the poor and oppressed. They *both* remain faithful to the Lutheran reforming tradition *and* critique that tradition for supporting the status quo or functioning as ideology. They *both* proclaim God's justification *and* work for human justice. In short, such individuals (and communities) are *both* radical Lutherans (deeply committed to a 500 year-old tradition) *and* Lutheran radicals (continually critiquing and reforming that tradition so that it serves those who need it most). Indeed, what makes each of the figures featured in this book so compelling is neither their proclamations of God's justification alone, nor their work for human justice alone, but rather the way they witness to the inseparability of both.

Søren Kierkegaard, for example, was never the "good Lutheran" that his family pastor wanted him to be. In fact, at the end of his life Kierkegaard railed against "the Lutheran establishment" for baptizing babies simultaneously into Danish culture and into the Danish People's Church. For him, such practices of the Lutheran establishment watered down commitment and made faith merely routine, as if being Lutheran meant little more than being Danish, or benign, or normal, or nice. Throughout his life, Kierkegaard relentlessly mused about how difficult—and how important—it was to become an authentic Christian in Christendom, especially when so many voices in church and dominant culture were telling you that everything was done in advance. Yet Kierkegaard was deeply Lutheran *even* and *especially* in his critique of the Lutheran establishment. He repeatedly called Lutherans back to the words and ways of Luther himself, who did not receive grace pre-packaged and gift-wrapped, but fought for it tooth and claw, like Jacob wrestling for God's blessing on the banks of the Jabbok (Gen 32:24–29).[7]

Or take Dietrich Bonhoeffer, the German Lutheran pastor and theologian who began his career with a fairly traditional reading of Luther's "doctrine of the two kingdoms"—commonly understood as the idea that one should follow Christ in "churchly" matters and the government in "political" matters. The problem was that Bonhoeffer's lawfully elected political leaders included Adolf Hitler, who became the Chancellor of Germany in 1933. With time, the very distinction between two kingdoms that led so many Christians to support the ascent of Hitler and National Socialism led Bonhoeffer to a life of theological musings intertwined with political resistance and, ultimately, martyrdom at the hands of the Nazis in solidarity with his Jewish brothers and sisters. According to Bonhoeffer, the central mistake of Nazi-supporting Christians (who were the majority!) was not that they obeyed the authority of Jesus on the one hand and political authorities on the other hand, but that they did not carefully enough distinguish the two, leading to *uncritical* or even *sacrosanct* support of the latter. One might say that his was a Lutheran critique of abuses in the Lutheran understanding of two kingdoms, just as he later draws on Luther's understanding of grace to critique Lutheran capitulation to "cheap grace." Such Lutheran critiques of Lutheran accommodation cost Bonhoeffer his life, but he knew what he was doing. His most famous book, *Discipleship*, begins by announcing that true, costly grace first cost Jesus *his* life and continues to bid Christians to "come and die."[8] Bonhoeffer answered that call.

7. Marty, *Martin Luther*, 25–27.

8. Bonhoeffer, *Cost of Discipleship*, 99. The newer translation renders Bonhoeffer's famous line thus: "Whenever Christ calls us, his call leads us to death." Bonhoeffer,

Less well-known outside theological circles is Dorothee Soelle, a mystic and activist who wrote and worked in Germany in the wake of Auschwitz. A feminist and liberation theologian, Soelle spent her career resisting in word and body all forms of authoritarianism and domination—from the Vietnam War and the arms race to sexism, racism, anti-Semitism, and first-world exploitation of the poor. She was ambivalent at best about church as an institution, including the Evangelical (Lutheran) Church in Germany into which she was baptized. In fact, among her most strident critiques of the Christian tradition was her objection to the very idea of an all-powerful—and quintessentially male—God who rules over history with perfect authority and invulnerability. For her, God as King or Lord or "A Mighty Fortress" easily leads to submission, but rarely if ever to human flourishing. But here's the rub: Soelle critiques such self-debasing praise of dominating power not only in the name of a fuller humanism, not primarily as a "post-Christian" feminist, and never as a strident atheist—as one convinced that any and all language about God and salvation necessarily becomes an opiate of the people, as Karl Marx (who influences Soelle considerably) would have it. Rather, she critiques dominant Christianity from the perspective of the suffering Christ, one who reveals a stranger sort of divine power, a "power made perfect in weakness" (2 Cor 12:9). Soelle thus embodies what Luther calls a "theologian of the cross," one who sees God fully revealed in Jesus's cross and in human suffering, as opposed to those "theologians of glory" who think of God in all-too-human terms. She, like Kierkegaard and Bonhoeffer before her, remains deeply Lutheran in her critiques of Christianity, including Lutheranism.

Kierkegaard, Bonhoeffer, and Soelle are deeply rooted in the theological vision of Martin Luther and also willing to critique that tradition and live it out in courageous and liberating ways. For each, the theological sources of revolutionary social change *share the same root system* as the proclamation of the Gospel, namely, the outlandish trust that God has acted decisively through Jesus to unveil a new kingdom and a new way of being in the world. Indeed, the primary payoff of considering Lutheranism from within this theo-socio-political tradition is that one finds therein not only *radical Lutherans*, those who want to get back to the roots of the tradition, but also *Lutheran radicals*, those who push against the neat boundary between church and society and show—with their writings, their actions,

---

Discipleship, DBWE 4:87.

and sometimes their lives—that God's gracious word frees one for social and political practices that are often subversive of traditional forms.

These are not the only radical Lutherans/Lutheran radicals. One might include the line of nineteenth-century German political philosophies spanning from Ludwig Feuerbach to G.W.F. Hegel to Karl Marx, who was baptized and raised as a Lutheran. More recently, German theologian Jürgen Moltmann rearticulates Luther's theology of a crucified God, a God in radical solidarity with the imprisoned, tortured, and executed.[9] Canadian theologian Douglas John Hall retrieves what he calls the "thin tradition" of Luther's theology of the cross over and against North America's quiet triumphalism and sentimentality.[10] Walter Altmann of Brazil argues that justification and justice go hand in hand—that the Lutheran emphasis on justification by grace through faith manifests itself in political activism, economic reforms, and other grassroots movements in Latin America today.[11] Many other teachers and writers—Mary Solberg, Deanna Thompson, Karen Bloomquist, Craig Nessan, Barbara Lundblad, Paul Chung, Cynthia Moe-Lobeda, Vitor Westhelle, Nadia Bolz-Weber, Heidi Neumark—to name just a few—immerse themselves in Lutheran theology but also teach about and participate in the healing of the world. The same is true for many of the young people drawn to Young Adults in Global Mission or Lutheran Volunteer Corps, for those involved in the care of creation through Lutheran outdoor ministries, or for those rethinking community and commitment at Holden Village. There are even movements such as *#decolonizeLutheranism* that strategically "counter notions of Lutheranism that are weighted by White Eurocentric models and theologies," and yet do so by doubling down on Lutheran understanding of God's justification *for all*, as expressed in Article IV of the Lutheran Confessions.[12]

It should be clear that we are using the word *radical* in a positive sense here. That is not always the case. Often, *radical* is wielded by those considered "normal" and moderate to raise a specter of fear and suspicion about dissenters and critics. The most recurring case over the past decade is the use of the term *radical Islamic terrorists* when referring to "extremists" who justify their violence by appealing to the will of God. *Islamic* and *terrorists* (not to mention *extremist*) are powerful and dangerous words in

9. Moltmann, *Crucified God.*

10. Hall, *Cross in Our Context*, 13.

11. Altmann, *Luther and Liberation.*

12. See http://decolonizelutheranism.org/our-beliefs/

themselves; their use—especially when juxtaposed—should raise questions about who gets to use them and toward what end. Adding *radical* to such phrases does not help to describe perpetrators of violence any better. Are there, for instance, *moderate* terrorists? If not, then what does *radical* add?[13] Sometimes dissident groups are able to reclaim the very words used against them, as Black Panthers in the 1960s were able to do.[14] Sadly, however, being dubbed *radical* proves to be a lot to get out from under, as the Black Lives Matter movement is presently experiencing.[15]

Given the perilous power of such language, four clarifications about our use of *radical* are in order. First, we are using the term as "insiders" to name a tradition that we know and respect. Each of the authors teaches about one or more of these Lutheran figures at a Lutheran college or university. Many of us also belong to (and sometimes lead) Lutheran congregations. It is thus a tradition that we treat sympathetically—although not uncritically. Second, our use of *radical* is meant to open up the careful investigation of issues related to faith, justice, and activism rather than to shut critical thinking down. In this sense, we use the word *in the reverse way* as those featured on contemporary cable news feeds. (To be clear, we intend no associations of the term with violence, legal or illegal.) Third, we are most interested in when, why, and how the two primary definitions of *radical* come together. That is, we will attend to how the deepening, or re-rooting, of a theological tradition can and has informed bold protest against the social, political, and cultural status quo. (Things get interesting when the status quo includes conventional, establishment Lutheranism; Kierkegaard, Bonhoeffer, and Soelle each use Luther and Lutheran theology to rethink and resist certain compromised forms of Lutheran culture and church.)

Finally, we assume that *radical* designates not only words and ideas but also courageous actions—in our case, actions that faithfully live into the final justice and jubilee announced by Jesus and that will even help bring it about. Karl Marx once quipped that "philosophers have only *interpreted* the world, in various ways. The point, however, is to *change* it."[16] The same

---

13. In fact, the word here functions almost entirely as propaganda; it further sidelines, scapegoats, and silences, making the acts of some utterly incomprehensible while justifying any measures taken against these outcaste "others." See the penetrating work of Butler, *Frames of War*, 152–56.

14. See Blake, "Black Panthers are Back."

15. Chasmar, "Greg Allen, Black Texas Police Chief."

16. Marx, "Theses on Feuerbach," thesis XI.

may be true of Christian theologians, Lutherans included. Admittedly, the radical Lutherans/Lutheran radicals investigated here are all considered theologians; their day jobs, so to speak, are to reason about God. Yet, their reasoning about God and God's kingdom also leads them to act on behalf of it, risking ridicule, imprisonment, and even death in the process. Only as such do they deserve the designation *radical.*

Roots and Shoots, and How This Book Develops

You are probably reading this book because you are connected to a Lutheran college, church, or social service organization, or have Lutheran friends, colleagues, or relatives. Maybe you have decided to attend a Lutheran college or university and this is the book that all students are reading over the summer. Maybe you are enrolled in one of the many "Lutheran Heritage" or "Luther and his Legacy" courses that are taught at almost every college connected to the Lutheran church. Maybe you teach at a Lutheran school and have been asked to read and discuss this book as part of your faculty development program, the kind of program my college calls "Augustana as Lutheran Education," or "ALE" for short. (Yes, we talk over beer.) Maybe your Lutheran church—or Methodist, Mennonite, or Catholic church, for that matter—has decided to commemorate the big anniversary of the Reformation in 2017 (which marks 500 years since Martin Luther's 95 Theses) and they've chosen this book to read and discuss. Maybe you picked it up to learn more about your Lutheran friend, who is an agreeable person but seems anything but radical.

Whatever brings you to this book, we hope you find it informative, provocative, and maybe even inspirational. By showcasing the intricate connections between the theological roots and countercultural shoots of Luther, Kierkegaard, Bonhoeffer, Soelle, and others, the book calls into questions our culture's prima facie divisions between devout religious "believers," those who want to "conserve" Christianity and other cultural traditions, on the one hand, and ostensibly secular or enlightened social critics and political "liberals," on the other hand. The best of the Lutheran tradition is simultaneously theologically traditionalist and socio-politically progressivist. Evangelical Christians (as followers of Luther were first called) hold firmly to their ultimate liberation by God through Christ *and therefore* are free to advocate for their neighbor's liberation in strategic ways.

What is more, whereas "radicals" are often imagined to be isolated individuals in their nonconformity, lone heroes who break away from tradition, this book points to a distinct historical line—a *tradition*—of radical Lutherans and Lutheran radicals. The figures who follow draw deeply from one another's writings as major theological sources. More importantly, their lives become something of an accumulating pattern that is itself patterned after a self-giving Christ (see Phil 2) and that inspires others to follow in turn. Thus, the five chapters of this book, while each focusing on a single radical Lutheran/Lutheran radical, also sketch out a theological tradition that overlaps with the church tradition called Lutheran but is not contained within it. If it helps, you might imagine the individual radicals here as aspen trees of the same grove. Aspens *look* like individual trees nestled closely together. But an ecologist or botanist or someone from Colorado will tell you that aspen groves actually comprise a single organism; what look like individual trees are actually shoots off the same, interconnected root system. So too with radical Lutherans: Those able to peek underground see that Soelle, Bonhoeffer, and Kierkegaard, as well as Luther, the Apostle Paul, and Jesus's early disciples, all grow out of the same soil. They share the same deep roots, shooting out in distinctive directions.

While this is a short book, a brief preview of each chapter and its author may help orient the reader:

In chapter 1: "Martin Luther: The Forgotten Radical," Samuel Torvend, Professor of the History of Christianity and endowed University Chair in Lutheran Studies at Pacific Lutheran University (Tacoma, Washington), puts Luther in his own historical context. He does so to show just how radical Luther's reforms were, especially when it comes to care for the poor and marginalized. Torvend argues that what Luther calls the first form of "righteousness" (or justification) is absolutely inseparable from the second, social form that righteousness takes when lived out in solidarity with the "hungry poor."[17] Once Christians have Christ as their righteousness, they "therefore seek *only* the welfare of others."[18] According to Torvend, Luther put this theology into practice, for example, by developing a common chest whereby the poor were offered no-interest loans from a community's common purse. So constitutive is the sharing with the receiving of God's gifts that Luther calls the Christian's unwillingness to share "robbery."[19] Tor-

17. Torvend, *Luther and the Hungry Poor.*

18. Luther, "Two Kinds of Righteousness," *LW* 31:299.

19. A similar sentiment is attributed to another radical, Dorothy Day: "If you have

vend thus calls for a re-investigation (and re-radicalizing) of Luther's early social-political-theological musings—a calling that Kierkegaard, Bonhoeffer, and Soelle help answer.

In chapter 2: "Søren Kierkegaard: Protesting the Lutheran Establishment," Carl Hughes, Assistant Professor of Theology at Texas Lutheran University (Seguin, Texas) and Secretary-Treasurer of the Søren Kierkegaard Society (USA), shows just how Lutheran Kierkegaard is *exactly* when he's critiquing Lutherans for selling out. Nineteenth-century Lutherans, according to Kierkegaard, have essentially turned Luther's fervent efforts at reform into an "ism"—into Lutheran*ism*—in a way that overlooks and avoids passionate human striving and discipleship. Kierkegaard thus tries to reintroduce the life-and-death strivings of Luther into a Lutheran establishment that confuses grace with latitude and privilege. While Hughes appreciates this ongoing reformation of the tradition, he also questions whether Kierkegaard's *radicalism* does not pass into an *overly-extreme prejudice* against everyday church communities and the common good.

In chapter 3: "Dietrich Bonhoeffer: Political Resistance in Tyrannical Times," Lori Brandt Hale, Associate Professor of Religion at Augsburg College (Minneapolis, Minnesota) and Secretary for the International Bonhoeffer Society (English Language Section), builds on the prior two chapters by showing how Dietrich Bonhoeffer also rethinks and radicalizes the good news of God through Christ in light of Hitler's Nazi Germany. On Hale's reading, Bonhoeffer initially subscribed to the Lutheran two-kingdoms "doctrine," but came to see that bifurcation of reality (into a "political" and an "ecclesial" realm) as providing insufficient leverage against Germany's political leadership, and also insufficient witness to the one reality redeemed by God through Christ. Bonhoeffer's critique of "cheap grace" likewise questions Lutheran assumptions by retrieving Luther's more radical vision. Admittedly, Bonhoeffer considers the possibility of being called to direct political resistance in ways that Luther would not and could not imagine. And yet, Hale traces how Bonhoeffer recasts Luther's dictum, "sin boldly," in socio-political form, and does the same with what follows: "but let your trust in Christ be stronger still."[20]

In chapter 4: "Dorothee Soelle: Lutheran Liberation Theologian of the Cross," Jacqueline Bussie, Director of the Forum on Faith and Life and

---

two coats, one of them *belongs* to the poor."

20. The full statement to Melanchthon is this: "sin boldly, but believe and rejoice in Christ even more boldly." Luther, "To Philip Melanchthon" *LW* 48:282.

Associate Professor of Religion at Concordia College (Moorhead, Minnesota), argues that Dorothee Soelle's theology both goes to the heart of Luther's understanding of knowing God through the cross of Christ, and presses far beyond what typical accounts of "Lutheran" might mean. On the one hand, Soelle remained ambivalent at best about the German Lutheran church, which to her had all the trappings of bourgeois and ideological Christianity. On the other hand, her own accounts of God—as hidden within the most "godless" forms of human affliction (including, but not limited to, that of Jesus)—can be read as a modern version of Luther's Heidelberg Disputation, where the reformer argued that only people who perceive God hidden in suffering deserve to be called true theologians.[21] Bussie thus shows how a thick strand of liberation theology takes its bearings from the "thin tradition" of Luther's theology of the cross, and yet radicalizes it in important ways.

Finally, in chapter 5: "You: Radicalizing Life's Calling," I (Jason Mahn, Associate Professor and Chair of Religion at Augustana College, Rock Island, Illinois) come to terms with objections to Lutheran understandings of vocation or calling insofar as they tend to sanction, legitimate, or "divine rubber stamp" the careers that we find satisfying. I take these objections to heart. While jobs and careers should be meaningful, and while even the most everyday task can disclose God's own work in the world, contemporary Lutherans and other Christians ought not to sacrifice our *primary* callings to do justice, become peacemakers, and to till and keep the soil (Gen 2:15) for the general legitimacy of any and every job. Despite the common reception, Luther's own understandings of calling and vocation do highlight the neediest and most vulnerable, including children, the sick and imprisoned, and even eroding topsoil, as those who point Christians toward justice. Attending especially to the primary calling to Adam in Genesis, I consider why and how vocations might be radicalized for care of the earth and all its inhabitants.

Lutheran Theological Terms—Some Help

Each of the five authors traces how certain Lutheran understandings of God and the world get extended and deepened (radicalized, you might say) by those within the tradition, including Martin Luther. While the authors introduce these understandings when they come to them, an overview of

21. Luther, "Heidelberg Disputation," *LW* 31:52.

some key Lutheran theological terms and themes might prove helpful at the start. The following paragraphs entail a very short primer in Lutheran theology; the italicized terms are included in this book's index in order to point toward subsequent discussions.

Central to Martin Luther's understanding of the Christian message is *justification by grace through faith.* Justification (or righteousness) concerns how one stands before or "lines up" with God. Luther came to understand that one is justified only and entirely by God's *grace,* that is, by God's sheer gift of acceptance, forgiveness, and love—indeed, of God's very self. *Faith* is the bold acknowledgement and reception of that gift. It follows that one is "saved" not by scoring moral or religious points but by being claimed and called by a loving God. While Luther often writes of justification or righteousness in this singular sense, he also writes about *two kinds of righteousness* in a treatise by that name.[22] Here, Luther makes clear that God's grace frees Christians from their own desperate attempts to secure their salvation, but then also to be for any and every neighbor who needs their help. Luther makes this same point when he writes of *the freedom of a Christian* in a famous sermon by that name.[23] God's grace *simultaneously* frees one from all despair and doubt *and* enables one to freely bind oneself to be in solidarity with others. Bonhoeffer (borrowing substantially from Kierkegaard), uses *"cheap grace"* to designate a *misinterpretation* of Luther's emphasis on free grace—one that essentially forgets the second form of righteousness or what Bonhoeffer calls discipleship. In preferring cheap grace, so-called Lutherans mistake grace as the empowerment to love and serve with latitude and license to do as little as possible.

Luther came to his understanding of grace and justification through his own experiences—especially his self-defeating attempts to win God's love through his own merits. Putting trust in himself only led to *Anfechtungen,* the German word that Luther used to describe the "spiritual trials" or "existential bouts" that accompany the manic focus on one's own capacities, rather than on God's grace and the neighbor's needs. So formative were these experiences that Luther (following the church father Augustine) largely defined sin as being *incurvatus in se,* or curved in upon oneself. While grace frees one from despairing self-regard, for Luther it never *displaces* sin (or doubt and trial) in the life of a Christian. Even grace-filled, faithful Christians remain throughout their lives *simul justus et peccator,*

22. Luther, "Two Kinds of Righteousness," *LW* 31:293–306.
23. Luther, "The Freedom of a Christian," *LW* 31:327–77.

simultaneously justified (or saintly) and sinful. However, even though sin remains, it no longer dictates one's actions or rules one's life. Indeed, Luther understood the freedom of a Christian to be so full and final that he once advised Philip Melanchthon (a fellow reformer) to "*sin boldly*"—that is, to act courageously, without obsessing over "the rules."[24]

While Luther's experiences shaped his theology, his understanding of God was founded on his interpretation of the Bible, which Luther regarded as everywhere pointing to Christ. *Sola scriptura* (Scripture alone) has thus become a motto of the Lutheran Reformation, along with *sola gratia* (grace alone) and *sola fide* (faith alone). Much of Luther's debates with the church hierarchy of sixteenth-century Christendom boils down to the question of whether we need Scripture to judge the church's teaching or need the church's collective wisdom to adequately interpret Scripture. (Luther argued for the former.) Luther also understood God's Word through the Bible to work in two broad ways: as law and as gospel, or what is sometimes called the *law/gospel motif*. God gives laws (or "the law") not only to maintain political order and teach one what is right (*the "first use" of the law*) but also to show one just how far one is from winning righteousness/justification on one's own, thus throwing one back on the grace of God (*the "second use" of the law*). This second (or "theological") use is most important to Luther because it drives a person to *the gospel*. (Gospel literally means the "good news" announced by Jesus, but for Luther, it includes the whole of God's unconditional love of those who do not "deserve" it.) Note that "law" and "gospel" do not name parts of the Bible (each is contained in the Hebrew Bible/Old Testament and each in the Christian New Testament). Rather, they name the way God's Word through Scripture *works* on people—primarily, by convicting them of their sin and then offering participation in the very life of God.

Related to Luther's regard for Scripture alone is his conviction that God must reveal Godself in order for humans to know God. Luther emphasized *revelation* (which means God's *self*-revelation) over-and-against late medieval conceptions of *natural theology*, or the idea that a person can know something of God through human reason and the empirical world. In his *Heidelberg Disputation* (1518), Luther argues that all attempts to know God by one's own lights risk becoming ideological; that is, they imagine God to possess the kind of power that certain humans (those *in* power) really claim for themselves, thus justifying their ways in the world. Over-and-against

24. See n. 20 above.

such *theologians of glory*, Luther calls for *theologians of the cross*, those who know God by looking to where God paradoxically chooses to "hide" God's self—especially in the cross and suffering of Jesus. That God remains hidden—a *deus absconditus* or hidden God—even and especially as God reveals Godself is something of a paradox in its own right.

Luther's emphasis on the cross makes it sound as though he is giving an *atonement theory* here, that is, an understanding of the way humanity is reconciled with God by the suffering, sacrifice, and/or victory of Jesus. But really, Luther's *theologia crucis* (theology of the cross), is about *theodicy* (broadly: an interpretation of suffering in light of God), and about *theology proper*, literally who God is and how we understand Her.[25] Because suffering and the cross remain privileged sites of God's self-revelation for Luther, some (such as Dorothee Soelle) connect his theology with *liberation theology*. Liberation theologians (most of which hail from Latin America or other non-first-world places) lift up God's good news *for the poor* in particular (see Luke 4:18). They thus speak of a "preferential option for the poor and oppressed." Liberation theologians will not claim that those with social, political, and economic power are not loved by God, but they do claim that understanding God's love and its relation to justice depends on being in solidarity with those who know God and grace with less risk of ideological self-justifications.

The same Lutheran emphasis on finding God among the lowly and suffering also leads Lutherans to see God in material and mundane things. Luther understood the *sacraments* to actually bear God. Unlike other Protestant reformers, he took Jesus's words, "this is my body," in their plain sense—as a promise that Christ was really "in, with, and under" the bread and wine that is consecrated during communion.[26] Extended beyond church practices, Luther's *sacramental theology* affirms that God is not located above and beyond the "stuff" of creation but in and through them. This evens out the status differential between those people and things

25. While I typically avoid gendered language for God, I use the female pronoun in this case (1) because it functions in our context just as Luther's language of finding God fully revealed on the cross of Jesus did for Luther—namely, to overturn typical connotations and underscore the intellectual and affective scandal of the Gospel; and (2) because male pronouns for God still function *ideologically* for many today—that is, they portray God and God's power in terms that parallel the power of males (and especially affluent, straight, white males), thus justifying the status and privilege of some over others.

26. The Lutheran understanding that Christ is really present "in, with, and under" the elements of a sacrament goes back to the Formula of Concord (1577), Article X, in Kolb, *The Book of Concord*.

typically considered "holy" or "godly" and those that seem mundane or even profane. Indeed, Luther writes of the *priesthood of all believers*, meaning that any person can disclose or mediate Christ to another person. He also repurposes the word *vocation* (from *vocare*, or "to call"). Whereas in the Middle Ages (and in many Catholic communities today), it was only nuns, monks, and priests who had a vocation, Luther understood all people to live out vocations or callings whenever they use their God-given gifts and stations in life to serve a neighbor in need. It follows that God is actively at work not only in the church but also in other spheres (family life, civil society, government, etc.). Luther thus writes of *two kingdoms*—the "spiritual kingdom" and the "worldly kingdom" or "kingdom of humanity." While God works in different ways through each, God is just as present and active in prisons and public schools as in cathedrals and confessionals.

These are some theological staples of the Lutheran intellectual tradition. A final term orients us directly to the narrative that follows. After Luther posted his 95 Theses on the door of Castle Church in Wittenberg and as he continued over the next 30 years to reform the church catholic, he never assumed that that task would be completed by him. The "Protestants"[27] who followed largely agreed. Over time, they developed the idea of *ecclesia semper reformanda est*, (sometimes shortened to *semper reformanda*) or, the idea that the Reformation church is always reforming itself. In the case of radical Lutherans/Lutheran radicals, ongoing reformation entails critically questioning the very tradition that is being deepened and extended. Ironically, then, the most incisive critics of status quo Lutheran Christianity make their bold protests by drawing deeply from that very tradition.

An Invitation

The authors of this book hope that you will read it discerningly and critically, but also generously and with an open mind—ready to think in new ways about a radical theological tradition that is always in danger of becoming merely "nice." We find very few niceties in the tradition that begins with Jesus's revolutionary politics, is emphasized in the Reformation, and then gets re-rooted in the writings and lives of Lutherans such as Søren Kierkegaard, Dietrich Bonhoeffer, and Dorothee Soelle. It is a tradition that

---

27. *Protestants* get their name from a group of princes who *protested* Emperor Charles V when he sought to reunite the Empire and shut down the Reformation. See Marty, *Martin Luther*, 151–52.

is lived out in mundane but countercultural ways through the vocations of countless Christians in all corners (and even flyover country!) of the United States no less than in twentieth-century Germany, nineteenth-century Denmark, or first-century Palestine. Whether you are studying this tradition as your own, are looking at it from an outsider's perspective, or even consider yourself another potential shoot from the root system, we hope you will dig deeply into this strange, fallible, beautiful, difficult, countercultural, and grace-filled tradition called Lutheran.

For Further Reading (and Viewing)

Altmann, Walter. *Luther and Liberation: A Latin American Perspective*. Minneapolis: Fortress, 1992.

Forde, Gerhard. *Justification by Faith: A Matter of Death and Life*. Mifflintown, PA: Sigler, 1990.

Luther. Directed by Eric Till. 2003. MGM. 2004. DVD.

Mahn, Jason A. *Becoming a Christian in Christendom: Radical Discipleship and the Way of the Cross in America's "Christian" Culture*. Minneapolis: Fortress, 2016.

Marty, Martin. *Martin Luther: A Life*. New York: Viking/Penguin, 2004.

McGrath, Alister. *Christianity's Dangerous Idea: The Protestant Revolution—A History from the Sixteenth Century to the Twenty-First*. New York: HarperOne, 2007.

Discussion Questions

1. What impressions of Lutherans or Lutheranism do you have? How do those match up against this book's focus on radical Lutherans and Lutheran radicals?

2. What's the difference between being radically Lutheran in Gerhard Forde's sense and being "Lutheranly" radical in more social and political ways? Does one of these come more easily to you, your college, or faith community? How so?

3. How are Søren Kierkegaard, Dietrich Bonhoeffer, and Dorothee Soelle "Lutheran" even as they critique major stands of the Lutheran church and Lutheran theology? Is Lutheranism a tradition particularly good at critiquing itself?

4. Should Christians be activists—taking clear stands in political and social debates? Why or why not?

1

Martin Luther

The Forgotten Radical

Samuel Torvend

Who was this man known throughout the world as the "father" of the Protestant Reformation? The answer to that question depends, of course, on the person answering it. To Lutheran pastors, Martin Luther (1483–1546) has served as the first minister in the Christian community that bears his name. To others, he is considered a biblical scholar whose intense study of Scripture led him to question the teaching and practices of late medieval Christianity, a questioning that contributed to the division of western Christianity. Professors in universities and seminaries see in Luther a theologian who dramatically changed the landscape of Christian faith and life, who offered a liberating view of God and God's relationship with humanity. Christian musicians have found in Luther the imaginative blending of ancient texts with contemporary tunes and have cherished his commitment to music as the greatest art. Pastor, biblical scholar, theologian, and musician: these are the images that have shaped the public perception of Luther and have guided that school of Christian spirituality called Lutheranism. Indeed, the many publishers of books on Luther tend to focus on his sermons, biblical commentaries, and vast theological writings. The colleges and universities associated with the Lutheran church carry the musical tradition of choral and instrumental works that sprang from the reformer's desire to create a community united in song.

What has remained on the margins of classrooms and worship spaces over the first five hundred years of Lutheran reform are the ways in which

Luther's experience *of life* contributed to the *revolutionary social reforms* he animated: reforms that have changed and continue to influence public life in profound ways. That leaders in Lutheran churches and schools may be unaware of Luther's economic, political, and social reforms is not surprising. In a recent survey of Lutheran congregational leaders, only 8 percent were aware of the fact that Luther had written about or promoted radical reforms in ecology, the economy, education, financial institutions, government, political leadership, and social assistance. While they were familiar with some of his sermons, his writings on two or three letters of St. Paul in the New Testament, his most famous hymn, "A Mighty Fortress," and a number of theological works, they had not been tutored in his life and the social reforms that sprang from his reflection on his life in light of the Scriptures. While Luther is hailed as the reformer who championed the Bible as the only trustworthy guide for Christian faith and life—*sola scriptura* ("Scripture alone")—isn't it possible that his life experience also served as a potent force in animating the powerful currents of reform that flowed from a small university far removed from the centers of financial, political, and religious power? If so, then let us consider his life and how his encounters with those who lived on the margins and those who exercised considerable social power converged in reforms that animate contemporary commitments to social justice.

A Father's Ambition Rejected

We have no way of knowing what went through the mind of Hans Luder as he rushed his newborn son to the Church of St. Peter and St. Paul only a few hours after his birth. We do know that the infant was baptized on November 11, the feast of St. Martin of Tour, and given the name Martin in honor of the fourth-century soldier who resigned his commission and eventually became a Christian bishop. Luder, like many others, believed that the Christian practice of water-washing an infant in the name of God would protect the newborn from evil spirits. In a time when large numbers of infants died within the first year of life, Christian baptism could offer solace to heartbroken and grieving parents; their child was somehow protected in the afterlife and waiting for them in what medieval artists portrayed as a heavenly city filled with light, joyful reunions, and happiness.

We also know that Martin's father was ambitious for his first-born son, an ambition that had transformed Luder from a poor man into a person of ample financial means. As the younger son raised on a farm, Luder could not inherit the family land and thus needed to leave home in order to find his way in the world. This left him close to impoverishment. Nonetheless, he was able to marry Margarethe Lindemann and start a family as he toiled in a copper mine. The ambition of the father fueled his desire to excel in business and send his son to school. Luder needed to be financially secure in order to do this, since education was reserved only for those who could pay the school fee. In time, Luder became a mine owner with prospects of expanding his successful enterprise. The young Martin was sent to school in Mansfeld, then Magdeburg, and finally Eisenach. While he studied hard and was viewed by his teachers as a bright student with a beautiful singing voice, Luther viewed his early education as "a taste of hell" devoted to rote memorization and the threat of punishment if he misbehaved or raised a question.

From uneducated poor man to laborer to mine owner, Luther's father had broken through the barrier of class, an astonishing achievement at the end of the fifteenth century. And yet economic security was not sufficient; he wanted more, especially for his son. Would it not advance the standing and fortunes of the family if Martin became a lawyer? And would not a career in law gain access to the nobility who were among the few who could pay legal fees? Wouldn't Martin the lawyer have connections to persons who could support his father's growing copper business? And in a world that knew nothing of pensions or state-supported social assistance for the elderly, wouldn't Martin's status and hoped-for wealth sustain his parents in their old age? While we have little idea what Luther wanted to study, we know that his parents were eager for him to enter a lucrative career that would bring them honor and security.

The young man entered the University of Erfurt in 1501 and completed a master's degree ("at that whorehouse of a school," as he called it). Bending to his parents' pressure, he prepared to enter studies in law. Then the unexpected happened: two of his closest friends died suddenly and terribly of the plague. And then Martin had a close brush with death when he accidentally wounded himself with a knife. These two experiences may well have caused him to reconsider the direction of his career path. Experiencing grief and its disorienting power, he was then easily alarmed by a thunderstorm as he returned from home to the university. Lightning struck close by and he found himself cowering on the ground, praying to St. Anne, the patron saint of miners, his prayer a desperate bargain: if you save me from death, I will enter a monastery and give my life to the church. As Martin would tell his father later in life, he was terrified of death and feared the judgment of God, a fear prompted by the belief that he had not been sufficiently spiritual to merit God's favor and eternal life. Did he have second thoughts about the vow he made to the heavens? After all, it was a promise made in fear. But Luther, having made the vow, was convinced that he could not break it.

To the utter surprise and frustration of his parents, he abandoned law school and entered the Congregation of the Observant Hermits of St. Augustine, a community of friars who were committed to the reform of their religious order. The Augustinians, one of many religious orders in late medieval Christianity, were guided by a rule of life written in 400 by Augustine of Hippo, a bishop and theologian. Like Luther, Augustine had also experienced a dramatic change in life, a change popularized through-out the Middle Ages in his autobiography, *Confessions*.[1] With considerable zeal, the earnest Luther dedicated himself to the practices of his reforming order, practices that were intended to distinguish the reformers from other Augustinians who were lax and lived in comfort. Not only did Luther fast on Fridays (in imitation of the hunger Jesus experienced on the day of his crucifixion), but also on other days during the week. Convinced that he had broken or would soon break the laws of God and the Church, he frequently sought a priest to whom he would make a thorough confession of his sins. He was especially attentive to the poor who requested food and drink for themselves and their children at the friary's door. He was fervent in prayer, spending many hours in the congregation's chapel, kneeling before the al-tar. In all this he was inspired by the words of Jesus: "Whenever you give alms, do not sound a trumpet before you . . . whenever you pray, go into your room and shut the door and pray to your Father . . . and whenever you fast . . . put oil on your head and wash your face, so that your fasting may be seen not by others but by your Father who is in secret ; and your Father who sees in secret will reward you" (Matt 6:2, 6, 17–18).

In all these practices, the young Luther was guided by the teaching of the late medieval church, a teaching that guided the Christian from this earthly life to union with God in heaven. Medieval theologians taught that the presence of the risen Christ was available to Christians through the sacraments: through the words and gestures inspired by the New Testament or directly commanded by Christ. These words and earthy rituals mediated

1. Augustine, *Confessions*.

the invisible but potent grace of God to those who desired to receive or be in favor with God. Rather than a static object that one possessed, the grace of God the Father or Christ the Son was considered a powerful energy that animated a Christian's life. But the theologians also taught that this divine energy should not be ignored or rest dormant in the Christian's life. Rather, one was responsible for using, for acting upon, the energy received in order to *demonstrate* one's commitment to Christ and the church—the people of God—and thus, in the end, be *rewarded* with eternal life. Through a life devoted to daily prayer; to attending church services; to receiving the sacraments of Holy Communion, Penance (confession and forgiveness), Healing, Marriage or Ministry; to giving alms to the poor; to going on a pilgrimage to a sacred site; to signing up for a crusade; to becoming a priest, monk, nun, friar, or sister, the Christian would gain merit in the sight of God and demonstrate his or her good use of the grace freely given. All this was from the hope that in the end he or she would receive what the Scriptures called the "crown of glory," or everlasting union with God, with the saints and martyrs, and with one's family and friends in heaven. Grace was given freely but one had to work hard to merit God's favor.

Is Christ a Judge or Advocate?

Luther grew up in a religious atmosphere in which Jesus Christ was frequently portrayed as the judge of the living and dead. Indeed, every Christian at every Sunday Mass would confess his or her faith in "one Lord Jesus Christ . . . who will come in glory to judge the living and the dead."[2] Such words struck terror in Luther's heart because he did not know if he would pass muster on the Day of Judgment. Indeed, he was surrounded by paintings in which "the blessed" were directed to the heavenly city and "the damned" to a fiery pit filled with monsters. Perhaps his imagination was stirred by the ongoing presence of the Black Plague—which most Europeans perceived as a terrible punishment for human sins. When Luther reflected on the failings of his life and the image of Christ the judge, he fell into despair. Indeed, late medieval church teaching claimed that a Christian must work hard "spiritually" to gain Christ's favor. This teaching troubled Luther, for when he asked his religious superiors: "How much must I do to gain Christ's favor and thus ensure eternal union with God and all that is good?" they responded: "We don't know. Do what you can and trust God's

2. The Nicene Creed, established in the fourth century.

25

mercy." Thus, Luther found himself living a terrible irony: he had given his life to God and the Church and yet he had grown to resent and even despise the very God to whom he had given his life. In his words, "I stood before God as a sinner troubled in conscience, and I had no confidence that my merit would assuage him. Therefore I did not love a just and angry God, but rather hated him."[3]

Luther received a temporary reprieve from his spiritual anguish in 1508 when his former religious superior, Johann von Staupitz, invited him to teach at a newly established university in the small town of Wittenberg in central eastern Germany. The son of an ambitious father, Luther lost little time in completing a degree in biblical studies, another degree in theology, and a doctorate—and did so in the span of four years. Having completed his studies, he was invested as a professor in the university faculty in 1512 and began teaching courses on individual books of the Bible. As he lectured on the Bible in Latin (the language of education, law, and commerce), he rigorously questioned the meaning of the ancient text. But that questioning was not only of academic interest; it was deeply personal. What meaning might this text hold, what counsel might it offer a young person beset with doubt and anxiety? Luther's personal dilemma—his sense that he was not good enough, not spiritual enough—pushed him to question the text and to seek a resolution to his doubts, what he called *Anfechtungen*, a miserable physical and psychic feeling.

In 1513, Luther began his lectures on the Psalms, a collection of poetic prayers that were sung each day in the Augustinian community. It was his study of the first few verses in Psalm 22 that caught his attention: "My God, my God, why have you forsaken me? Why are you so far from helping me, from the words of my groaning? O my God, I cry by day, but you do not answer; and by night, but find no rest" (22:1–2). In these few words Luther recognized his own distress for he, too, felt forsaken, unable to obtain any answer to his spiritual anguish. His religious superiors and mentors could not help; he prayed, he "groaned," but heard no answer from God. And then Luther remembered this: that in dying, Jesus had quoted these same words from the Psalm: "'Eloi, Eloi, lema sabachthani?' which means, 'My God, my God, why have you forsaken me?'" (Mark 15:34). Luther wondered: was it possible that the image of Christ as a remote and demanding judge was inaccurate? Did this brief passage from one of the gospels not offer a much different portrayal: one in which Jesus also experienced the absence of God

3. Luther, "Preface to the Complete Edition," *LW* 34:336–37.

at this most critical moment in his life? And could it be, wondered Luther, that if the central figure in the Christian story experienced such terrible suffering in the past, would he not be attentive to human suffering in the present? Luther experienced doubt and anxiety, a visceral sense that he had not worked hard enough to gain God's favor. His body suffered punishing spiritual exercises; his thoughts were marked by uncertainty; his soul was bereft of comfort: his experience mirrored the experience of the forsaken Jesus. Indeed, Luther began to wonder if God were present to him, not in all his fervent efforts to please a stern heavenly judge, but with him at the lowest point of his life. If God were present there, feeling the anguish of his children and God's child, Jesus, would such an experience not mark a radical departure from the idea that God was aloof from human limitation, suffering, and death? Indeed, Luther knew that every artistic image of the risen Christ displayed the wounds left by the nails and spears that marked his body in death. Between his own experience of suffering and his study of ancient texts, his perception of the central figure in Christian history had begun to shift, bringing a measure of peace.

Questioning Established Authority

And yet his anxiety did not suddenly dissolve. Having completed his lectures on the Psalms in 1515, Luther began a course of study on Paul's letter to the Christians at Rome, a letter written in the mid-50s of the first century. As he prepared his lectures, he was arrested by Paul's discussion of "righteousness," a term that had bedeviled Luther for years. "I am not ashamed of the gospel," Paul wrote, "[for] it is the power of God for salvation to everyone who has faith, to the Jew first and also to the Greek. For in it the righteousness of God is revealed through faith for faith; as it is written, 'the one who is righteous will live by faith'" (Rom 1:16–17). As a student, Luther had been taught that the "righteousness of God" was the power of God to condemn and punish sinful human beings. It was a term, Luther wrote, that terrified him. After all, he grew up in a spiritual system that instructed people to work zealously to become "right" with God, to "justify" themselves before God and so avoid condemnation. Paul, in the first century, offered a much different viewpoint. Paul wrote that it is God who brings people into a right relationship with God out of sheer love for them—by grace alone—and thus frees them from needless worry about their eternal destiny and the commonly-held view that one must work diligently to gain divine favor. This Pauline insight from the letter to the Romans began to liberate Luther from his profound anxiety:

> At last, by the mercy of God, meditating day and night, I gave heed to the context of the words, namely, "In it the righteousness of God is revealed, as it is written, 'He who through faith is righteous shall live.'" There I began to understand that the righteousness of God is that by which the righteous lives by a gift of God, namely by faith. And this is the meaning: the righteousness of God is revealed by the gospel, namely, the passive righteousness with which a merciful God justifies us by faith, as it is written, "He who through faith is righteous shall live." Here I felt that I was altogether born again and had entered paradise itself through open gates. There a totally other face of the entire Scripture showed itself to me.[4]

What, then, of the church's admonition to work hard, to do the "best" one could with the "spiritual energy" offered by Christ in the sacraments: in Holy Baptism, Holy Communion, and Confession? Was it really better to become a monk, a nun or a priest—professions considered "holier" than the work of a miner, housewife, student, professor, or ruler? Could donating money to the church, going on pilgrimage to a sacred site, or giving handouts to the poor actually contribute to one's status in the eyes of God? *If God and God alone justified regardless of one's condition in life,* then the desire to claim the privilege of one's gender, ethnicity, or social status was ruled out. No human condition or effort could be used to gain favor with God. Thus, the Pauline insight possessed a profoundly egalitarian implication that would prove unsettling in the stratified culture and religious community of sixteenth-century Germany. Luther insisted that God is the primary actor in the act of justification, received passively by the person at Holy Baptism. Indeed, Luther would never depart from or diminish this emphasis on what a merciful God does for human beings in order to liberate from an innate and sole focus on the self.

At the same time, the act of justification possessed a social dimension. The Christian is called to grow in loving and maturing responsibility to others in the world. In effect, Luther's insistence that all persons become fundamentally equal to each other through Holy Baptism signaled a departure from a hierarchically-ordered society (the few at the top with much or all power and the rest dependent upon the few). From his understanding there emerged a more democratic ordering of society in which the many

4. Ibid., 337.

use their gifts and skills for the common good of their communities because their labor benefits others. No longer needing to work hard to gain God's pleasure, the Christian could now tend to the alleviation of suffering and injustice in *this* world. The justification whose source is God flows into acts of justice by maturing Christians who take seriously their responsibilities to others.

As he reflected on his new understanding of God's relationship with human beings, Luther began to call into question much of what he had been taught and had accepted as "normal" throughout his life. He had come to the root, the *radix*, of his problem. Indeed, if the Pauline teaching on justification by grace was the foundation of Christian life, wouldn't other dimensions of church teaching and practice need to be critically examined and reformed? Luther became both energized by his "discovery"—for it brought immense relief to his anxious soul—and terrified because the very insight that brought him consolation also challenged the teaching and practice of the most powerful social institution of his time: the Roman Church, governed by the pope to whom Luther had vowed obedience when he was ordained a priest. Relief and terror were mixed in Luther once he recognized that to question church teaching and authority was to question the palpable presence of the church in all dimensions of human life—from birth registry to death and inheritance laws, from the regulation of marriage and marriage contracts to the curriculum of universities, from the silencing of laywomen in church to the consecration of monarchs by bishops or popes. To call into question what most people knew had existed for centuries and was considered "normal" was to risk a figurative slap on the hand, to risk silencing by one's religious superiors, to even risk death by fire (at the stake) or water (by drowning) if one refused to be obedient to the established religious authorities.

In 1517, Luther offered a range of statements to the faculty of his university concerning a religious practice he thought unhelpful to Christians. In 95 carefully worded theses, Luther called into question the sale of spiritual favors that were believed to free a Christian from divine punishment before and after death. This practice supported the late medieval notion that at death one's soul entered a purgative state to prepare it for union with God in heaven. One's "time" in this process, commonly called purgatory, could be lessened through the purchase of a spiritual favor, a pardon, from the church. The letters of pardon, called indulgences, were approved by Pope Leo X, and sold by salesman who made a handy profit for church officials. Luther was deeply critical of the profit gained at the expense of the poor, who could not afford such pardon letters. He also recognized that such sales gave the clear impression that one needed to buy what should have no price attached to it. Luther began to recognize that the late medieval church sponsored a "spiritual economy" in which Christians who had the funds to invest could reap spiritual benefits after death. This church-sanctioned practice not only obscured but also contradicted what Luther had discovered in his study of the New Testament, namely, that the forgiveness offered by God is free, unconditional, and abundant. Furthermore, he could find no evidence in the New Testament or early Christian writings to support the notion that a Christian needed to work hard to gain God's favor *after* death! Luther argued that death ends everything:

> The dying are freed by death from all penalties, are already dead as far as the canon laws are concerned, and have a right to be released from them . . . Any truly repentant Christian has a right to full remission of penalty and guilt, even without indulgence letters. Any true Christian, whether living or dead, participates in all the blessings of Christ and the church; and this is granted him by God, even without indulgence letters.[5]

Luther diagnosed a twofold problem in the sale of indulgences. On the one hand, the sale of spiritual favors had no scriptural basis and twisted the free forgiveness offered by God into a moneymaking scheme that benefitted a few wealthy church leaders. On the other hand, the practice was an instance of economic injustice in that the vast majority of the population—the impoverished or the working poor—was exhorted to purchase such indulgences in hopes of releasing the suffering souls of their relatives from years and years of torment. The problem was that Luther not only questioned the sale of indulgences and the wrongful profit wrung from the poor, but also questioned the person who had approved their sale: the supreme leader of all Christians in Western Europe, a man who spent lavishly on himself, his friends, and the arts, and who spent the Vatican Treasury into bankruptcy. Thinking that his theses would enliven a discussion at a faculty meeting in little Wittenberg, he was surprised to learn that the document—a radical critique of a profit-motivated spiritual sales program—was sent to Rome and soon made its way to the pope's desk. Suddenly, the name of the priestly professor from a small university in Germany was on the lips of many in the Vatican.

5. Luther, "Ninety-Five Theses," *LW* 31:26, 28–29 (theses 13, 36–37).

The Social Dimension of Justification by Grace

The hard work of examining an ancient text for its deeper meaning had eased Luther's anxiety, freed his conscience, and then catapulted him into notoriety as he began to ask more and more troubling questions. With other humanistic educators in Wittenberg and throughout Western Europe, Luther discovered a path to personal renewal and social reform through the study of languages (Hebrew and Greek), ancient literature (the Bible), and history (early Christianity). Indeed, the New Testament, only recently received in its original Greek form, appeared to Luther and other professors as a charter of reform for church and society. Now interpreted through the lens of justification by grace alone, the Bible became the mirror through which the Wittenberg reformers examined and tested the teachings and practices of the late medieval church. If a contemporary practice or claim was not clearly supported in Scripture, it was rigorously examined and frequently rejected. Such questioning was not received well. For those who benefitted from the status quo, who wanted things to remain exactly as they were, the growing number of Luther's publications (which sold out quickly across Europe) were received as an assault on their most cherished assumptions. Shouldn't he be silenced and ordered to stop publishing? After all, he had made a vow of obedience when he joined the Augustinians.

In short order, Luther was asked by his religious superiors to prepare an explanation of his theses that would be given in Heidelberg during the annual meeting of the reform-minded Augustinians in April 1518.[6] But rather than cooling down, Luther did just the opposite. He not only upheld his earlier criticisms, but he was also emboldened by his study of Scripture enough to offer a cutting criticism of the entire philosophical foundation of medieval theology.[7] The move lead to division; many of his Augustinian colleagues supported Luther, while others considered his ideas dangerous. Death threats followed and Luther's supporters even suggested that he have bodyguards if he were called to another meeting outside of Wittenberg to defend his reforming ideas.

---

6. It is in this Heidelberg Disputation that Luther famously distinguishes "theologians of glory" from "theologians of the cross"—a distinction to which subsequent chapters of this book will return. Luther, "Heidelberg Disputation," *LW* 31:52–53 (theses 19–21).

7. To be clear, Luther was not the only scholar who criticized the monumental work of Thomas Aquinas (1224–1274), the medieval theologian who integrated Aristotelian philosophy and Christian theology. It must also be noted that Luther never read Aquinas' *Summa Theologica*, only later commentaries on the work.

In the same year, Luther preached on the two forms of Christian righteousness, setting forth the teaching on justification by grace. The first and primary form

> is alien righteousness, that is the righteousness of another, instilled from without. This is the righteousness of Christ by which he justifies through faith . . . This righteousness, then, is given to men [sic] in baptism and whenever they are truly repentant . . . Just as a bridegroom possesses all that is his bride's and she all that is his . . . so Christ and the church are one spirit.[8]

Luther both connects and contrasts this "alien" righteousness to a second form, or what he calls one's proper righteousness:

> The second kind of righteousness is our proper righteousness, not because we alone work it, but because we work with that first and alien righteousness . . . This righteousness consists in love to one's neighbor . . .[9]

Here Luther offered a Pauline interpretation of the command to "love the Lord your God with all your heart . . . and to love your neighbor as yourself" (Mark 12:29–31). In effect, Luther argued that God is always advancing toward human beings with grace and mercy. This "advance" continues in the world of daily life through Christians called to love and care for the neighbor in need. No longer, argued Luther, need one assist the neighbor in order to gain supernatural advantages (while using the neighbor for one's own personal gain). Rather, the Christian is called to share that which he or she has already received: the grace and mercy of God. In other words, the theological claim—Christ's righteousness is offered freely and without condition—holds a social mandate: "As love and support are given you [by Christ in Holy Communion], you in turn must render love and support to Christ in his needy ones. You must feel with sorrow all . . . the unjust suffering of the innocent, with which the world is everywhere filled to overflowing. You must fight, work, [and] pray."[10] While the theological claim can be *distinguished* from its social implication, the two *cannot be separated*. Luther was clear in his argument: what Christ gives freely must be extended into the world through the actions of Christians, through their commitments to the wellbeing of others. God does not need this action but

8. Luther, "Two Kinds of Righteousness," *LW* 31:297.

9. Ibid., 299.

10. Luther, "The Blessed Sacrament," *LW* 35:54.

the neighbor who suffers does. In other words, the abundant love of Christ becomes palpable on this earth and in human life through the works of justice and peace: "We work with the first and alien righteousness." Indeed, Luther could never have imagined that "love" be reduced to one's feeling for another person. Christ was not put to death because he had loving feelings for others (though he did have these feelings), but because his love energized his commitment to the "life, health and salvation" of others, a commitment made tangible in word and action.

Rather than spend one's life and energy working to gain the favor of God and the reward of immortality in heaven, Luther argued that the Christian could direct those energies toward life on earth, toward the amelioration of suffering and the diminishment of injustice. *This was a complete reversal of the spiritual world in which Luther was raised.* Rather than striving for union with God, he argued, the teaching on justification by grace claimed that God is the One who seeks out humans wherever they find themselves in the world. To say the least, his critics recognized the radical nature of this teaching and insisted on more hearings and trials. They asked that he be dismissed from his religious order unless he rejected his writings. Others pushed for his excommunication from the church and his execution by the state. One of his critics called him a heretic, "a leper with a brain of brass."[11] The faculties of the Universities of Cologne and Louvain condemned his writings. In 1520, Pope Leo X condemned Luther's writings and gave him sixty days to reject them or suffer excommunication along with all of his supporters.

The Great Democratization—and Subversion

Less than three months after he received word of Leo's condemnation, Luther published an appeal to the nobility of Germany, asking them to support his reform of church and society. Indeed, he had all but given up on the Pope, his Roman bureaucracy, and many of the church officials in his native Germany. In this first major reforming document, Luther upended 500 years of Christian thought and practice.[12] In contrast to the medieval division of society into two categories—"spiritual" (religious professionals) and "temporal" (all other Christians)—Luther argued that Christian baptism demolished any stratification between "holy" and "not so holy," creating

11. Silvestro Mazzolini de Prierio, as cited in Bainton, *Here I Stand*, 77.
12. Martin Luther, "To the German Nobility," *LW* 44:115–217.

a community marked by spiritual equality in which the members could choose and dismiss their own leaders. Grounded in his study of Paul's New Testament letters and the practice of early Christians, Luther argued for the deconstruction of a hierarchical church. Some were left gasping at his argument: how could a peasant be the spiritual equal of a priest or a pope? How could an uneducated housewife or a marginally literate shopkeeper select their religious leaders? Didn't one need expertise, education, and rank to make such important decisions? Why give the majority of people—poor people—voice in the selection of priests, pastors, and bishops? Luther thus asked for the end of an organization controlled by one person and his appointees, many of whom gained appointment through bribes.

He also asked that papal monopoly on the interpretation of the Bible come to an end and that each Christian community have access to the Scriptures in their own language so that every person could read and interpret the foundational text of Christianity. However, the Bible was published almost exclusively in Latin rather than German, the language of Luther's students and the parishioners of the university church he served. Thus, he began the process of translating the entire Bible into German. In 1522, the New Testament was published with artistic images created by Luther's colleague and confidant, Lucas Cranach. In 1535, the entire Bible was translated into German by a group of university scholars working with Luther. Indeed, Luther is praised in Germany today as the creator of the modern German language.

This project was rooted in the core Lutheran teaching on "Scripture alone," or *sola scriptura*. The Bible served as the tutor in Christian faith and life. Since the impulse for reform was first discovered by Wittenberg scholars in the New Testament writings of the apostle Paul, the Bible as a charter for ongoing reform would need to be given to the community as a whole, rather than controlled by those few versed in Latin. This was a remarkably subversive project; it allowed German Christians to read the entire Bible in their own language for the first time, and in their reading discover persons, events, and ideas that were previously hidden. Here was Deborah, the judge of Israel, and Mary, the student of Jesus—images that inspired women followers of Lutheran reform to contribute to the movement.[13] Here were the

13. Consider, for instance, Elisabeth Cruciger, Argula von Grumbach, and Katharina Schuetz Zell, three women who were caught up in the reform movement emanating from Wittenberg. Their public speaking and writing, newly discovered in the twentieth century, was inspired by their study of the many women in the Bible who were leaders, warriors, judges, preachers, teachers, apostles, and benefactors. Indeed, they called into

people of Israel calling out for liberation from an oppressive society ruled over by a monarch, what many reformers considered a mirror of their own situation. Here was Jesus driving moneychangers out of the Temple, a potent image of cleansing and reform that emboldened the reformers and led some to call Luther the "temple cleanser" and the German Hercules.[14]

And yet with the German illiteracy rate between 80–90 percent in the sixteenth century, what good could the translation effect if only a few could read it? Thus, early Lutheran commitments to universal literacy, expressed in the reform of education, emerged. The pressing need for literacy prompted Luther to ask that all municipal councils in Germany establish and maintain schools in which both girls and boys could receive education in reading, arithmetic, and religious instruction. This was the first time in human history that a nation was called to educate boys and girls from all socio-economic classes. It was the first time in history that a nation was called to provide education for all children through taxation of all citizens. It was, to say the least, an astonishing achievement given the amount of resistance from working parents who saw no need to educate their children and from wealthy merchants and landed nobility who saw no need to support the poor. And yet, within 50 years of the proposal, over 300 schools were established throughout those parts of Germany that had accepted what came to be called the "Lutheran" reform. At no previous time in human history had anyone made the radical proposal to transform an illiterate nation into a body capable of reading the Bible and, of course, any other text. No longer the preserve of a few educated elites, this translation, publication, and literacy project became the first step in the democratization of knowledge.

"Greed is an Unbelieving Scoundrel"

In 1523, one year after completing his translation of the New Testament, Luther was asked to assist the small German city of Leisnig as it fully embraced the changes promoted by the Wittenberg reformers. The city leaders had followed the reformers' appeal to suppress all monastic communities in the area. This was done for largely theological reasons. Now released from

question the silencing of laywomen that had obtained in the medieval centuries. See Stjerna, *Women and the Reformation*.

14. Hercules (Greek *Herakles*) was the mythic figure who embarked on Twelve Labors, defeated opponents, and gained what many thought were rewards out of his reach.

his vows to the Augustinians, Luther claimed that religious communities of monks, nuns, friars, and sisters gave the clear impression that a vocation to religious life was superior and holier than the foundation of Christian baptism in which all Christians shared. He did not ask for the destruction of the monasteries and convents, as did other reformers. Rather, in a moment of moderation, he suggested that those who chose to remain in their religious community be allowed to do so until death or voluntary departure. Once vacated, the buildings could be transformed into schools or hospitals. Addressing one problem, however, created another. With the suppression of religious houses, the thousand-year-old network of social assistance, sustained by monastic and mendicant communities, was dismantled in one fell swoop.

The "Lutherans" at Leisnig asked Luther to assist them as they faced persons who were homeless, hungry, impoverished, unemployed, chronically ill, orphaned, or elderly without family to care for them—an incredible catalogue of need. If, at one time, monks and nuns had served as the charitable and merciful face of the church, the suppression of their communities brought this to an end. Should the needy be left to fend for themselves? No, argued Luther. If the social dimension of justification by grace is love for the neighbor, no one in need could be overlooked or pushed to the margins. Attention to and care for the most vulnerable persons in one's society was neither an option to be entertained when time allowed nor a social work to be handed off to the few volunteers, the few faith-based organizations, the few non-profits that needed to raise funds for their work. Love for the neighbor meant little unless it took concrete form in social policy that actually changed the conditions in which the vulnerable lived. From this urgent need there emerged a body of legislation call the "church order," which transferred responsibility for social assistance to city councils and congregations, funded by taxes and directed by laypersons. This was both a religious and civic reform. There was resistance to the project: wealthy town members saw little reason, religious or humanitarian, to pay the tax, make a donation, or establish funds to assist their fellow citizens. In despair, Luther wrote, "Greed is a disobedient and unbelieving scoundrel"—a ravenous consumption of what rightly belongs to all.[15]

The protest against such greediness was the establishment of a common chest where the people of Leisnig would make donations of food and money, and into which tax money would be deposited. A board of ten

---

15. Luther, "Ordinance of a Common Chest," *LW* 45:170.

directors supervised the distribution of these gifts to those in need. Prior to any distribution, the directors (drawn from peasant farmers, shopkeepers, city council members, and nobles) would meet with persons requesting funds, get to know them, discern their need, and chart a course of assistance. Donations, taxes, and the work of directors became the first state-funded and supervised initiative in human history that included food assistance for the hungry, job training for the unemployed, healthcare for the sick and the elderly, housing and education for abandoned children, and shelter for the homeless. In effect, the people of Leisnig were inspired by the social dimension of justification by grace and Luther's reform of the Christian congregation to create the first program of social assistance. Their legislation, the church order, became the model for all other Lutheran initiatives in Germany, the Nordic countries, the Czech Republic, and the populist states in the United States where Lutherans settled in large numbers.

Luther not only shifted social assistance from monastic communities to local government and congregations of laypersons (itself an unprecedented move in the sixteenth century); he also wondered why there was such opposition to an ethic of care for the hungry poor and children in need of education. Was it greed, the "ravenous consumption of what rightly belongs to all"? Luther prayed that Christians would be delivered from the "gaping jaws of avarice"—a mouth perpetually opened, waiting to consume more, a hunger within the soul that is never satisfied. Greed knows no limit, he claimed. It possesses an addictive property that grasps for more money, more possessions, more personal status, and more property. And yet it only deepens what Luther called one's curve toward the self-alone,[16] a narcissism that loves neither God nor neighbor. He heard the merchants saying: "So long as I have my profit and satisfy my greed, of what concern is it to me if it injures my neighbor in ten ways at once?"[17]

Luther had little difficulty bringing to light the power of greed in business dealings: "These [thieves] sit in their chairs and are known as honorable, upstanding citizens while they rob and steal under the cloak of legality."[18] Yet his ire was also directed at political leaders: "We might well keep quiet here about individual petty thieves since we ought to be attacking the great powerful arch-thieves with whom lords and princes consort

---

16. Recall from the Introduction Luther's favored definition of sin as being curved in upon oneself, or *incurvatus in se*.

17. Luther, "Trade and Usury," *LW* 45:247.

18. Kolb, *The Book of Concord*, 417.

and who daily plunder not just a city or two, but all of Germany."[19] Rulers are charged by God to ensure justice and equity as guardians of the law and as protectors of the people: "It is their duty to use their duly constituted authority in punishing the injustices of the merchants and preventing them from so shamefully skinning their subjects."

And yet politics and exploitative economics were often in cahoots. In Luther's words, "I hear that [the princes] have a finger in [collusion with monopolies], and the saying of Isaiah [1:23] is fulfilled, 'Your princes have become companions of thieves.' They hang thieves who have stolen [little] but do business with those who rob the whole world and steal more than all the rest."[20] Political leaders were susceptible to bribery from powerful interest groups; they were prone to serve their own avaricious interests, placing personal gain above care for their most vulnerable citizens.

As Ricardo Rieth points out, "Luther did not consider any social or professional class greedier than the others. He intended, instead, to identify and condemn greed in functions fulfilled by all members of all classes (*Stände*)."[21] It comes as no surprise, then, that in Luther's commentaries on the seventh commandment ("You shall not steal," Exodus 20:15), he speaks of the many who are plagued by greed: day laborers, workers, servants, artisans, burghers, butchers, shoemakers, farmers, tailors, beer-makers, owners of trading monopolies, church leaders, magistrates, and princes. All persons live within the tension between the inward curve where avarice grows and the power of grace to turn one in generosity toward the neighbor in need. Price manipulation, price fixing, charging exorbitant interest rates, appropriation of land for personal or corporate rather than civic and public use, accepting bribes to thwart the regulation of abusive business practices, the ever-present yearning for more and more with no sense of limitation or sufficiency, the eager desire for some measure of social mobility—all these practices and aspirations wreak havoc and mock care for the common good. The worst effects of greed can be curbed through government regulation of the banking industry and monopolies, the investigation of price-fixing and prosecution of the law, outlawing abusive loan practices, and citizen protest against misappropriation of land.[22]

19. Ibid.

20. Luther, "Trade and Usury," *LW* 45:271–72.

21. Rieth, "Luther on Greed," 166.

22. In Luther's writings on trade and usury (the practice of taking interest on a loan), he writes extensively about the economic system in which he lived, a form of mercantile capitalism that was expanding into the Western Hemisphere through the imperialist

The Wittenberg reformers were accused of abandoning biblically pre-scribed good works and placing inordinate emphasis on passivity in the presence of God's grace. The reformers contested this criticism by insisting that passivity in grace led to the absolute necessity of working for the good of one's neighbor. At the behest of Luther, they upended the notion that one must be charitable in order to gain God's favor. They insisted on care for others as the advance of grace into daily life: charity benefitted the neighbor in need and could diminish the misery in which people found themselves. But who would get upset about charity? Would even the most aggressive of Luther's opponents disagree with his insistence on "faith active in love"? Probably not. But publicly condemning the actions that *created* human misery was another matter, for such condemnation was leveled against the rulers, the owners of business monopolies, the bankers, and the merchants who had supported the reform, a reform that had released them from pay-ing taxes to the papal treasury. Luther said: "I have been asked and urged to touch upon financial evils and expose some of them so that, even though the majority may not wish to do [what is] right, at least some people may be delivered from the gaping jaws of avarice . . . Well do I know that only a few will follow my advice."[23] Perhaps he was correct.

A Radical?

In contemporary Germany, Luther is praised as the father of modern edu-cation, with his theological project set to the side. In countries influenced by Protestantism, he is known as the first to break away from the medieval form of Catholicism. In light of his refusal to reject his writings—while claiming that he was bound solely to Scripture and his conscience—some historians consider him the great champion of the individual, one of the first "early moderns." On the other hand, his vitriolic writings on women, peasants, the Jews, Anabaptists, other reformers, and the Catholic Church have made him *persona non grata* among some Christians and many schol-ars in the academy. Still others, deeply skeptical of Roman Catholicism, the matrix in which Luther's spiritual quest was formed, see him as the

---

conquests of Spain and Portugal, soon to be followed by Great Britain and France. Luther was profoundly distrustful of mercantile capitalism. Its one motive—the accrual of un-regulated and unlimited wealth for the individual or the corporation—was, in his view, an addiction that would demand one's obedience and loyalty, one's faith.

23. Luther, "Ordinance of a Common Chest," *LW* 45:176.

great bearer of a truth unavailable to other forms of Christianity and other religions. Luther has been all these things and more. But was he a radical, a term used frequently in academic and political discourse?

Luther was not satisfied with diagnosing the symptoms of a problem. If, for instance, an individual or a group harmed or abused others, the person or group could be punished through the administration of the law. But for Luther, punishing an abuser or a criminal was not sufficient; he wanted to get to the root, the *radix*, of the problem: Why do suffering and injustice course through human life, suffering and injustice which he himself experienced? In no uncertain terms, he suggested that human beings are focused on themselves, are curved in upon themselves, to the exclusion of others and their Creator. Indeed, he also came to recognize that systems and institutions created by human beings produce suffering and sanction injustice, neither of which are intended by God. He thus held forth the claim that only God has the power to transform human life. The deeply rooted problem begged for a "radical" response. That response, for Luther and his reforming colleagues, was the person of Jesus Christ who offered his liberating power freely, without condition, to anyone and everyone. For Luther, there was no such thing as a self-made human being who could boast in his or her prowess and skill. All is given freely by God. But with such generosity comes serious responsibility: "For you are powerful," wrote Luther, "not that you may make the weak weaker by oppression, but that you may make them powerful by raising them up and defending them."[24]

Rather than focus on one's eternal destiny, the Christian is called to follow Christ into the world, a world in need of love and justice: not one without the other. As the twentieth-century Lutheran martyr, Dietrich Bonhoeffer wrote, the Christian is called to see life with "a view from below," from solidarity with the vulnerable and the powerless.[25] Thus, the Christian is called act in the world, to engage the economic, political, and social fabric that shapes, often unconsciously and subtly, much of life and to discern in this world the ways in which love for the neighbor becomes the promotion of justice. You have been made just, wrote the reformer, so that you may become an advocate for others who live with injustice.[26]

24. Luther, "Two Kinds of Righteousness," *LW* 31:304.

25. The full quotation is as follows: "We have for once learned to see the great events of world history from below, from the perspective of the outcasts, the suspects, the maltreated, the powerless, the oppressed, the reviled, in short from the perspective of the suffering." Bonhoeffer, *Letters and Papers from Prison*, DBWE 8:52.

26. Such might be a summary of the whole of Luther's "Two Kinds of Righteousness,"

Upon hearing of his death in 1546, many throughout Germany and Western Europe proclaimed Luther the *Propheta Germania*: the prophet of Germany. Who is the prophet? Is he or she not the one who serves as the voice of God, diagnosing the injustice that dwells in society and offering an alternative marked by life, health, and wholeness? Pastor, Scripture scholar, theologian, and musician: yes to all these images. But set next to them, can we not add the unsettling presence of the passionate prophet, the revolutionary, and even the radical?

LW 31:293–306.

For Further Reading

Lindberg, Carter, and Paul Wee, eds. *The Forgotten Luther: Reclaiming the Social-Economic Dimensions of the Reformation*. Minneapolis: Lutheran University Press, 2016.

Luther, Martin. "Two Kinds of Righteousness," (1519). *LW* 31:293–306; *BTW*, 134–40.

Moe-Lobeda, Cynthia D. *Resisting Structural Evil: Love as Ecological-Economic Vocation*. Minneapolis: Fortress, 2013.

Rieth, Ricardo Willy. "Luther on Greed." In *Harvesting Martin Luther's Reflections on Theology, Ethics, and the Church*, edited by Timothy Wengert, 152–68. Grand Rapids: Eerdmans, 2004.

Torvend, Samuel. *Luther and the Hungry Poor: Gathered Fragments*. Minneapolis: Fortress, 2008. Reprint, Eugene, OR: Wipf & Stock, 2017.

Discussion Questions

1. How does the economic/political/ecclesial context into which Luther was born compare to our own? Which reforms to that worldview do we now assume to be customary or normal? Which are needed now more than ever?

2. In "Two Kinds of Righteousness" and elsewhere, Luther argued for the inseparability of an individual's reception of God's grace and her work for social justice. Do most Christians consider these inseparable today? If not, why not?

3. According to Torvend, one important result of the Lutheran Reformation was the first state-funded initiatives for food assistance, job-training, health care, and so forth. Do you find state-sponsored policies and programs to be more or less important than the efforts of individual Christians or congregations? Which are more "radical"—and in what sense?

4. Many today assume that the Christian faith is perfectly compatible with various economic systems (for example, a global free market economy). How does Luther's distrust of the emerging mercantile capitalism of sixteenth-century Europe challenge these assumptions? How do you respond?

2

Søren Kierkegaard

Protesting the Lutheran Establishment

Carl S. Hughes

It is February 5, 1854, a date near the end of Søren Kierkegaard's short life (1813–1855). The bishop of Zealand in the Danish state Lutheran church, Jacob Peter Mynster, has just died. Befitting his place and prestige, he is being given an elaborate official funeral in Vor Frue Kirke ("Our Lady Church") in central Copenhagen. Out of protest, Søren Kierkegaard is not attending.

Lutheranism has been the official religion of Denmark since 1536, when King Christian III converted the realm to the faith of the Reformation. Once a critical and subversive force that challenged the status quo, Lutheranism has now become the status quo itself. Pastors are civil servants, state employees. At their ordination, they promise to serve both Christ and the state—as though the interests of the two could never conflict. The baptism of babies is mandated by law. Denmark embodies a Lutheran version of what has long been known as "Christendom"—the unification of the political, social, and religious spheres under the umbrella of state-sponsored Christianity. For the first centuries of Christianity's history, following Jesus was a risky and potentially seditious act. Christians were a minority community, and their theology frequently challenged the foundational assumptions of the Roman Empire. Thousands of Christians were persecuted and even put to death for their faith. Similarly, in the sixteenth century, Martin Luther risked his life by questioning the teachings of the Roman Catholic

Church, making himself an outlaw in the Holy Roman Empire.[1] But those times now seem to have long since passed. In nineteenth-century Denmark, being Christian—being Lutheran—seems as simple as being Danish.

In Vor Frue Kirke, Hans Lassen Martensen—a rising Danish pastor who would become Mynster's successor as bishop—preaches a glowing eulogy for the deceased bishop, calling everyone to imitate the faith of this "true guide."[2] Martensen goes on to proclaim Mynster a "truth-witness"— indeed, a link in the "holy chain" of truth-witnesses stretching back to the first apostles of Christ.[3] Martensen probably never gives this rhetorical flourish a second thought. But when Kierkegaard gets wind of it, the words make his blood boil.

In the coming year and a half, right up until his death, Kierkegaard undertakes what has come to be known as his "attack on Christendom"— a virulent denunciation of Danish state-sponsored Christianity. Once the subtlest of literary writers, Kierkegaard now writes only in terse newspaper articles and pamphlets, which have the character of hand grenades. In January of 1855 he declares that "Christianity does not exist at all" in Denmark. Indeed, he claims the situation is worse than if no one even claimed to be Christian:

> We have what could be called a complete inventory of churches, bells, organs, offering boxes, collection boxes, hymn boards, hearses, etc. But if Christianity does not exist, then the existence of this inventory is so far from being Christianly of benefit that instead it is much more dangerous, because it so very easily occasions an erroneous view and the erroneous conclusion that if there is such a complete Christian inventory then there is naturally also Christianity.[4]

Churches, church bells, collection boxes, hymn boards, hearses—Denmark has all of these in amble supply. Yet possessing this inventory amounts to nothing more than going through the motions of Christianity, according to Kierkegaard. He insists that even though Denmark purports to be "a Christian nation . . . not a single one of us is in the character of the Christianity of the New Testament."[5] He dismisses the Lutheranism around him as nothing

---

1. See chapter 1 above.
2. Kierkegaard, *The Moment*, KW 23:359.
3. Ibid.
4. Ibid., 35.
5. Ibid., 36.

but "playing at Christianity" and "making a fool of God."[6] He focuses his ire particularly on the Danish clergy, whom he accuses of profiting from this charade. He translates Jesus's warning to beware of "those who like to go about in long robes" as, "beware of the pastors! Above all, beware of the pastors!"[7] He argues that Denmark's "silk-and-velvet" clergy are engaged in a shady ecclesial business of "forgery" and "swindling."[8] Having long since thrown restraint to the wind, he goes so far as to denounce the pastors as "cannibals," who live fat and happy off the blood and struggles of true Christians in ages past.[9]

For Kierkegaard, Martensen's description of Bishop Mynster as a "truth-witness" demonstrates that neither he nor anyone else in Danish Lutheranism has a clue what being a witness for Christ involves. The Greek word for witness is *martyron*, from which we get our English word *martyr*, meaning someone who is killed for his or her faith. In contrast, Mynster deftly climbed the ladder of ecclesial power by espousing a gospel to which few would take offense—least of all those in power. He lived in a grand residence provided by the state and belonged to the Copenhagen elite. No doubt someone like Martensen would ask how it could be otherwise in Denmark, a Christian nation. Will a Christian society not naturally reward true followers of Jesus? From Martensen's perspective, the age of martyrdom is ancient history, and—God be praised—the powers that be are now firmly on the side of Christ.

In his "attack on Christendom" and throughout his career, Kierkegaard denounces this alliance between Christianity and the status quo. He believes that Christ and true Christianity always come into conflict with the powers that be—whether these are societal, governmental, or ideological. Any church that declares itself an ally of the status quo has clearly sold its soul. So when a relatively sympathetic reader pleads with him to cease his extreme attacks now that he has made his warning clear, Kierkegaard responds by saying that his goal is not to ring a fire alarm, but to ignite a fire—and to see that it keeps growing. He notes that Jesus "came to cast fire upon the earth" (Luke 12:49), and says he wants to do the same.[10]

6. Ibid., 32, 30.

7. Ibid., 197.

8. Ibid., 43, 129.

9. Ibid., 321–23.

10. Ibid., 51.

Metaphorically speaking, this arsonist's goal is to burn Christendom to the ground.

We can certainly agree that Kierkegaard merits the title "radical," right? Nonetheless, we may also wonder whether he is perhaps *too* radical for our comfort. The statements quoted above may seem to careen past radicalism to religious extremism, insofar as they advocate a kind of violence, however metaphorical, against the established order. Our present age has no short- age of religiously sanctioned violence and talk of martyrdom, and we know that the consequences of this are tragic. So to what extent can Kierkegaard's radicalism really be associated with the spirit of Christ? Indeed, in what sense can he even be described as Lutheran, given his condemnation of the Lutherans all around him?

I will argue in this chapter that Kierkegaard does merit the titles "Lu- theran" and "radical" in the fullest and most deeply Christian sense of both terms. We will see that over the course of his career Kierkegaard advances his critiques of Luther, Lutherans, and Lutheranism in the name of some of the deepest principles of Lutheran theology. More importantly, we will see that his radicalism is motivated by a passionate commitment to Jesus and the radical love that he embodied. Kierkegaard believes that the God re- vealed in Jesus challenges every worldly status quo. Through his varied and extensive body of writings, Kierkegaard sets out to inspire even Lutherans to do the same.

The Making of a Lutheran Radical

The circumstances of Søren Aabye Kierkegaard's birth and childhood do not auger the formation of a radical. He was born on May 5, 1813, to one of the wealthiest families in all of Denmark. His father had built a successful mercantile business, in addition to benefiting from some lucky investments and inheriting considerable wealth. Because of the family fortune, Kierke- gaard never had to work an ordinary job. His sole occupation was to be a writer—in his words, "a singular kind of poet and thinker,"[11] "a poet of the religious."[12]

Perhaps Kierkegaard exercised this vocation in such a radical way be- cause the circumstances of his childhood were not as comfortable as they first appear. He was the youngest of seven children, but only he and his

11. Kierkegaard, *Without Authority*, KW 18:165.

12. *JP* 6:6511 (1849), p. 234.

older brother Peter Christian lived past the age of 33. His father, Michael Pedersen Kierkegaard, was a melancholy, strict, and severe man. Despite his eventual prosperity, he grew up poor in Jutland, a hardscrabble agricultural area of western Denmark. One day as a child, as he was tending his family's sheep upon a cold and damp moor, he cursed God for having given him such a miserable lot. To the very end of his life, he seems to have feared recompense from God for that insolent act. Moreover, after his first wife died in 1796, he impregnated his servant girl before the period of official mourning had ended, and this too fed his sense of guilt. He married the servant, and she went on to be the mother of all his children, including Søren. But melancholy and anxiety (today we would say depression) were Michael's constant companions. They became Søren's as well.

Because his father was very religious, Kierkegaard grew up attending two church services every Sunday: the Danish state Lutheran service in the morning and the pietistic Moravian Brethren meeting in the evening. Both Kierkegaard and his older brother Peter Christian pursued university educations in theology, though one brother did so a good deal more enthusiastically than the other. Peter Christian completed his theological examinations in a typical period of three years. He became a pastor in the state church and eventually a bishop. Søren, in contrast, took a full decade preparing for his theological exams. In a letter to a cousin in 1835, he describes the whole business of studying theology as distasteful and boring: "As far as little annoyances are concerned, I will say only that I am starting to study for the theological examination, a pursuit that does not interest me in the least and that therefore does not get done very fast."[13] What *was* Kierkegaard doing during this time? A Danish historian has calculated that during the year 1836, Kierkegaard spent more on books, clothing, restaurants, and tobacco than the average university professor earned in a year.[14] He was passionate about music, theater, and the arts but rarely attended church. He seems for much of the 1830s to have been a theology student—and perhaps even a Christian—in name only.

Like many young people during this phase of their lives, Kierkegaard was searching for who he was. In a famous journal entry from this period, he writes:

> What I really need is to get clear about *what I must do*, not what I must know, except insofar as knowledge must precede every act.

13. *JP* 5:5092 (1835), p. 23.
14. Garff, *Søren Kierkegaard*, 102–3.

What matters is to find a purpose, to see what it really is that God wills that *I* shall do; the crucial thing is to find a truth which is truth *for me*, to find *the idea for which I am willing to live and die.* Of what use would it be to me to discover a so-called objective truth, to work through the philosophical systems so that I could, if asked, make critical judgments about them . . . of what use would it be to me to be able to formulate the meaning of Christianity, to be able to explain many specific points—if it had no deeper meaning *for me and for my life?*[15]

Several of the central themes of Kierkegaard's future authorship are compressed in this youthful paragraph. There is his fixation on subjectivity, his search for a truth that is "truth *for me.*" (We will return to this subject soon.) Kierkegaard scorns the "philosophical systems" that many of his professors consider the height of intellectual sophistication. Unless he can determine "their deeper meaning *for me and for my life,*" he considers them trivial. He is more interested in the question of *how* he should live than in *what* he might claim to know. Further, he already intuits that the truth to which he will devote his life will not make it easier, but more challenging. He seeks a truth for which he is willing not only to live, but also to die. At the time of this writing, this truth seems not yet to have found Kierkegaard. But by the time he begins his career as a Christian author some eight years later, it most definitely has.[16]

Two major events intervened in Kierkegaard's life between 1835 and the publication of *Either/Or,* the book that inaugurates the body of work he later calls his "authorship." The first was the death of his father in 1838. In the wake of this loss, Kierkegaard began preparing in earnest for his theological examinations; he passed them with flying colors in 1840. He then spent a brief period in a pastoral seminary in pursuit of ordination to the ministry, but he quickly discerned that this path was not for him. Instead, he enrolled in the *magister* program (the equivalent of today's Ph.D.) in the field of philosophy, and he completed his dissertation in little more than a year's time.

The second seismic event in Kierkegaard's young life was his engagement to Regine Olsen, a girl of sixteen, in September 1840. Many of Kierkegaard's love letters to Regine from the time of their engagement survive, and they seem to present a picture of a happy couple. Yet Kierkegaard

15. *JP* 5:5100 (1835), p. 35.
16. For more on vocation or calling, see chapter 5 below.

decided to break off this engagement about a year later. This choice was a source of extraordinary pain for both of them—perhaps even more for Kierkegaard than for Regine. She went on to marry a respectable Danish government minister, but Kierkegaard never pursued any further romantic relationships. In his journal, he reflects almost obsessively on his history with Regine until the very end of his life. He eventually dedicates the entirety of his authorship to Regine and leaves her all his worldly possessions upon his death.[17] Traumatic as the breakup was for Kierkegaard, the experience provided the emotional rocket fuel that gave liftoff to his authorship, which commenced less than two years later.

Kierkegaard the Author

On February 20, 1843, a very unusual book arrived at Copenhagen bookstores. It looked nothing like a conventional work of modern theology. It was a set of two heavy volumes titled *Either/Or*. It did not even purport to be by Søren Kierkegaard but presented itself as a collection of papers compiled, edited, and introduced by a certain "Victor Eremita." The first volume, the "Either," consists primarily of essays by a young man whom Eremita simply calls "A." His writings are focused on art, worldly pleasure, and romantic relationships. On their face, they seem to offer a largely nihilistic worldview. The second volume, the "Or," contains a pair of sober letters written to A from an older, more conformist friend, a judge named William. He admonishes A to marry and to become a Christian—two paths that, to his bourgeois mind, amount to basically the same thing. Curiously, although the book's title seems to promise a black-and-white choice between right

---

17. The precise reason why Kierkegaard ended his relationship has always been mysterious. In his journals, he sometimes suggests that breaking up with Regine was the most loving thing he could do for her, perhaps because he did not want to burden her with his family's propensity to depression. At other times, he suggests that he needed to remain single in order to devote himself fully to his vocation as a Christian writer. At other times, he presents his decision not to marry as a willful rejection of the straightjacket of bourgeois society. Modern scholars have sought still other explanations: perhaps Kierkegaard was gay, or had a venereal disease, or suffered from some form of sexual dysfunction. Ultimately, however, Kierkegaard himself warns that such explanations are doomed to failure: "After my death no one will find in my papers the slightest information (this is my consolation) about what really has filled my life. No one will find the inscription in my innermost being that interprets everything" (*JP* 5:5645 [1843], p. 226). As we will see in the next section, Kierkegaard does not write in order to disclose his inner life, but to cause others to consider their own.

and wrong, neither of the two volumes presents anything close to authentic Christianity as Kierkegaard conceives it. What is the purpose of a book like this? Many of *Either/Or*'s initial readers assumed that it was nothing more than a virtuosic literary feat, with little underlying religious significance. Yet Kierkegaard later insists that every word of this book (and of the many equally idiosyncratic works that follow it) serves a Christian end.

Rather than presenting the truth about Christ and Christianity directly, *Either/Or* taps you on the shoulder and asks *you* to reflect on *your* relationship to Christ. What exactly do *you* think of Judge William? Is he really the sort of Christian *you* want to be? Or are you beginning to suspect that his comfortable certainties have compromised something fundamental about what following Jesus means? Might he (and *you*) have anything to learn from that passionate pagan, Aesthete A? Kierkegaard calls this sort of writing "indirect" communication—writing that is oriented toward a fundamentally "subjective" end. Understanding what he means by these terms is vital to appreciating his radical vision of what true Christianity involves.

Subjectivity, Indirect Communication, and the Passion of Faith

Fundamental to Kierkegaard's project as a Christian writer is his opposition to all "objective" interpretations of Christianity. When Kierkegaard was writing, the philosophy of G. F. W. Hegel (1770–1831) was fashionable in Copenhagen, promising a new sort of comprehensive knowledge about the world, including religion in all its forms. Kierkegaard opposes himself to this and every other objective presentation of Christianity because he sees them as cheapening true faith.

When Kierkegaard condemns Danish society for equating Christianity with an inventory of religious "objects"—all those bells, organs, offering boxes, and hearses—he is mocking one very crassly objective understanding of what being Christian means. Yet the inventory of objects with which Christians are tempted to equate faith can be intellectual rather than physical. In our time as in Kierkegaard's, Christians often equate *faith* with *belief*—usually an entire inventory of *beliefs* about God, Jesus, morality, and so forth. One must believe that God created the world, that Jesus was divine, that God offers forgiveness through Jesus, and so forth. In contrast, Kierkegaard rejects the notion that having the right ideas about God makes one Christian. From his perspective, intellectual beliefs are as worthless as religious paraphernalia if they don't reshape who one is and how one lives.

Faith for Kierkegaard is about how one relates oneself to God as a living and breathing human being—as a *subject*, in philosophical terms. Faith must be lived in the first person rather than talked about in the third person. After all, in the gospels, it is the *demons* who are the first to *know* that Jesus is the Messiah, yet this "objective" knowledge does them no good.[18] Kierkegaard writes in that early journal entry that he seeks a truth "which is truth *for me*," one "*for which I am willing to live and die*." He wants his readers to seek the same for themselves.

Instead of depicting faith objectively as knowledge or belief, Kierkegaard describes it in subjective terms as a "passion." Think for a moment about an interest you are passionate about. If you are passionate about playing the cello, for example, then people are likely to say that you devote your "heart and soul" to it. To be sure, you have a good deal of objective knowledge: you can recite the names of famous composers and cellists, demonstrate the finger positions for all the notes, and play a repertoire of pieces from memory. But by itself, this knowledge is not what makes you passionate about the cello. Your passion comes from that sense you have of how much there is about playing the cello that you *don't know*. Your passion is what motivates you to constantly strive to get better, no matter how good you already are. It is what makes you willing to make sacrifices and even suffer for the sake of your art. It is your sense that playing the cello is less a deliberate choice than a calling. It is your feeling that you wouldn't really be yourself without it. Kierkegaard wants us to think of faith in similar terms—as a yearning and striving that can only be inhabited from within. This is a fundamentally "subjective" conception of faith because it is about who you are and how you live, not a mere checklist of beliefs or paraphernalia.

Kierkegaard draws many of his favorite metaphors for faith from romantic relationships, one of the preeminent arenas of earthly passion. Like many medieval mystical authors, he often uses imagery of longing and desire to portray a Christian's relationship to God. As he conceives it, faith is more like the experience of falling in love than that of knowing a scientific fact. Throughout his writings, he depicts a variety of earthly lovers—happy and jilted, star-crossed and starry-eyed—to portray what the life of faith involves.[19] He suggests that the Bible is best thought of as a love letter, rather

18. See Mark 1:34; Matt 8:29; and Luke 4:41; compare Jas 2:19.

19. See for example: *Fear and Trembling*, KW 6:85–107; *Philosophical Fragments*, KW 7:25–35; and *Point of View*, KW 22:34.

than as a tome of history or doctrine.[20] Instead of saying that God satisfies human longing, he writes that God longs to be in relationship with each of us and wants us to respond with ever more passionate desire.[21]

Kierkegaard likes the imagery of longing and desire because it emphasizes that faith is not a matter of knowledge or choice. As we all know, what provokes romantic desire is, at least in part, the *otherness* and *mystery* of the beloved, and we can never fully explain the attraction. Kierkegaard believes the same is true with faith. Any God that we as human beings can claim to understand is not really God. Further, Kierkegaard emphasizes that God's incarnation in Jesus makes God less comprehensible, not more. He affirms the enduring "paradox," or unthinkable contradiction, in God's self-revelation in Christ. Who has really understood the claim that Jesus was fully human and fully divine? Does the notion that the creator of the cosmos became embodied in a poor carpenter, who was executed by the Roman state, "make sense"? Rather than describing faith as a rational choice, Kierkegaard portrays it as a "leap" into the "absurd." If love is blind, as the proverb says, then the passion of faith is even more resistant to rational control. Kierkegaard encourages us to think of God's self-revelation in Jesus as less like a scientific treatise and more like a beloved's alluring but enigmatic smile, which beckons us into a passionate relationship even though—or precisely because—we do not understand it.

Lutherans have long been tempted to depict faith in decidedly dispassionate terms as an inventory of objective beliefs. Yet it is important to recognize that, when they do this, Lutherans are deviating from Luther's own deeply subjective vision of what faith is. Luther frequently asserts that Christian doctrines are meaningless if they do not become true "for you." When Kierkegaard writes in the early journal entry quoted above that he is seeking a "truth that is truth *for me*," he is actually echoing one of Luther's most cherished phrases. Luther maintains that it is worthless to believe that Jesus died for the sins of the world or is present in the sacrament of Holy Communion as mere abstractions. What matters for both Luther and Kierkegaard is that Jesus died for *your* sins and offers himself to *you* at the altar.

Kierkegaard and Luther are united in insisting that faith is a subjective matter, but they do tend to depict faith's subjectivity in different ways. Whereas Kierkegaard portrays faith as passionate longing, Luther describes

20. *For Self Examination*, KW 21:26–30.
21. *Christian Discourses*, KW 17:251–61.

it first and foremost as *trust*. One of Luther's favorite images for faith is that of an infant who trusts his or her mother. This trust is certainly not the product of rational choice, as though the baby were saying to the mother: "I've considered all my other alternatives, and you seem to be my best shot at survival. I guess I'll just have to trust you." Rather, an infant's trust is a pre-rational, instinctive, and thus passionate response to being loved. Luther uses this image to argue that God's love always finds us before we even know to look for it. Faith for Luther is a matter of trusting God's love rather than seeking to justify ourselves. For his part, Kierkegaard sometimes speaks of faith in terms of trust, but, as we will see later in this chapter, he worries that this depiction of faith becomes "objectified" in Lutheran Christendom. He believes that Lutheran trust can function as little more than a permission slip for spiritual complacency. By recasting faith's subjectivity in terms of love, longing, and desire, he endeavors to revive the relational conception of faith that is at the heart of Luther's own theology.

Kierkegaard's commitment to the subjectivity of faith leads him to insist, perhaps surprisingly, that he *is not* a Christian—only someone in the process of striving to *become* one.[22] This is not a judgment about his faith in comparison to that of others—as though he were saying that he himself is not a Christian, but four of the eighteen other residents of his street actually are. Rather, he is saying that it is wrong to think of faith as a thing or object that one either does or does not "have." Faith for Kierkegaard is not a binary, on/off, either-you-have-it-or-you-don't sort of thing. Because faith is a subjective passion, it is always "in process"; it always has room to grow. Just as love for another person must renew itself day after day, so too Kierkegaard believes that faith is a continuous journey. Johannes de Silentio writes in *Fear and Trembling* that faith is "a task for a whole lifetime," not something "acquired either in days or weeks."[23] Rather than offering the confidence that one *is* a Christian, faith means striving to *become* one more and more each day.

Kierkegaard's subjective orientation is what leads him to deny that groups and institutions of any kind can be Christian. For him, faith's journey always takes place along an individual path. We will consider potential objections to this aspect of Kierkegaard's theology at the end of this chapter. For now, let us simply appreciate that Kierkegaard believes that just as only

---

22. See for example *The Moment*, KW 23:340–42; *Point of View*, KW 22:43; *Concluding Unscientific Postscript*, KW 12.1:617, 360–87.

23. *Fear and Trembling*, KW 6:7.

an individual can fall in love, so too only an individual can have faith. He insists that any faith claimed by a group is always something objective—a set of doctrines or identity markers disconnected from personal commitment. At the end of *Fear and Trembling*, Johannes de Silentio writes that because faith is "the highest passion in a person," no generation ever progresses collectively beyond any other in matters of faith.[24] Just as it would be ridiculous to say that we today are better at being in love than people in Shakespeare's time, so too it is wrong to say that it is easier (or more difficult) to have faith in our era than at the time of Jesus. As fundamentally subjective experiences, being in love and having faith present essentially the same challenges to every individual in every time and place. Faith required a leap of Jesus's first followers—and it requires a leap today. Faith meant coming into conflict with the status quo in the first century—and it is equally risky today. Because of sin and the chasm between the human and the divine, Kierkegaard denies that any society is ever going to progress to a point where being a Christian will be easy and supported by the world. Each individual must walk the road of faith for her- or himself.

Kierkegaard's subjective understanding of faith is what leads him to reject conventional theological writing and to experiment with various forms of "indirect communication." We all know that any effort to describe the experience of falling in love in objective prose will be imperfect at best. More importantly, no matter how true to life a description of falling in love may be, it cannot make *you* fall in love *yourself*. Kierkegaard believes that communication about God will always be limited in a similar way. He is acutely sensitive to the danger of confusing discourse *about* faith with the lived reality *of* faith. As a result, he thinks that there is little point in trying to build up faith "directly" by writing lengthy tomes of doctrine. Instead, his goal is to build up faith "indirectly" by getting you to examine your faith for yourself. He models his method of indirect communication on the conversation of Socrates, the ancient Greek philosopher who taught by asking questions rather than by promoting his own theses. Socrates liked to describe his philosophical role as that of a midwife—helping other people give birth to their ideas. In *Either/Or* and many other books, Kierkegaard envisions himself as doing something similar. Rather than telling you the meaning of Christianity, he spurs you to think about what Christ means for you and for your life. His goal is to fan the flames of your own relationship to God.

24. Ibid., 121.

For the next several years after *Either/Or*, Kierkegaard published numerous books under a variety of false names, even though virtually everyone in Copenhagen knew that he was the ventriloquist. He also published devotional texts under his own name, but most of the blockbuster titles from 1843–1846 are attributed to pseudonyms. *Fear and Trembling* is by Johannes de Silentio; *Repetition* is by Constantin Constantius; *Philosophical Fragments* is by Johannes Climacus; *Stages on Life's Way* is edited by Hilarius Bookbinder; and so forth. Kierkegaard took the integrity of his various personas surprisingly seriously. "In the pseudonymous books," he writes, "there is not a single word by me." Indeed, he asserts that "if it should occur to anyone to want to quote a particular passage from the books, it is my wish, my prayer, that he will do me the kindness of citing the respective pseudonymous author's name, not mine."[25] Like most Kierkegaard scholars, I follow his request to refer to the authors of the pseudonymous books by their given names. Still, no matter who the author of these books is said to be, they all disrupt the objective certainties of Christendom and solicit ever more passionate faith.

Walking in Jesus's Footsteps

Considered in isolation, Kierkegaard's language of subjectivity may seem to imply that faith is a wholly inward matter—all about an individual's private relationship to God, with little significance for how one actually lives. Yet nothing could be further from the truth as Kierkegaard sees it. In the second half of his career, Kierkegaard begins to publish more extensively under his own name, and the focus of these later works is on how the passion of faith transforms how one lives. Echoing the Epistle of James's assertion that "faith without works is dead" (Jas 2:17, 26), Kierkegaard insists that faith requires imitating Jesus in every arena of one's life.

Kierkegaard's book *Works of Love* (1847) is one of his most beautiful writings from this period. He argues that all authentic love for God manifests itself concretely in the world as love for human beings. He denies that love for God could ever compete with love for human beings, since the former expresses itself precisely as the latter. "If you want to show that your life is intended to serve God," he writes, "then let it serve people."[26] To be

25. *Concluding Unscientific Postscript*, KW 12.1:626–27.

26. *Works of Love*, KW 16:161. Compare here Torvend's analysis of Luther's "Two Kinds of Righteousness" in chapter 1 above.

sure, the idea that Christians are called to love human beings is not exactly unheard of in Christendom. The command to "love your neighbor as
yourself" is enshrined throughout the Old and the New Testaments and is
a staple of Christian preaching. Yet just as Kierkegaard believes that Christendom hijacks the notion of faith, so too he believes that it trivializes the
command to love one's neighbor as oneself. Always seeking to find an easy
way out, Christendom equates Christian love with what human beings already do naturally: love their family, friends, and romantic partners—those
to whom they are naturally inclined. Kierkegaard is not opposed to this
sort of love, but he believes that you do not have to be Christian or have a
command from God to practice it. God certainly did not have to enter the
world in the person of Jesus to teach it. Instead, what Jesus taught was the
following: "If you love those who love you, what credit is that to you? For
even sinners love those who love them . . . But love your enemies . . . expect-
ing nothing in return" (Luke 6:32). Kierkegaard insists that the distinctive
challenge of Christian living is to love those to whom one is *not* naturally
inclined: the ugly, the vulnerable, the needy, the hateful, the undeserving,
the enemy. Loving in the image of Christ means loving those who cannot
or will not ever pay us back.

Christians are sometimes tempted to believe that following Jesus is
a recipe for success and happiness. Many in Kierkegaard's time espoused
what is known today as the "prosperity gospel": the notion that being
Christian is a route to wealth, prestige, and security. Yet in *Works of Love*
and other texts from this phase of his career, Kierkegaard insists that the
reality is just the opposite. The more we love in the image of Christ, the
more we are likely to suffer for it.[27] After all, society's reaction to Jesus was
to arrest, torture, and kill him. Kierkegaard does not believe that followers

27. It is worth noting that in 1846 Kierkegaard underwent a traumatic experience
that fed his interest in the themes of suffering, persecution, and martyrdom and their
connection to Christian life. A Danish satirical newspaper called the *Corsair* began making sport of his literary celebrity through a campaign of ridicule against him, mocking
his writings and persona in articles and cartoons. It depicted Kierkegaard as a self-righ-
teous dandy parading around Copenhagen in flamboyant but ill-fitting clothes. More
woundingly, it mocked his cherished theme of subjectivity as nothing but narcissistic
self-absorption. Suddenly, strangers began bursting into laughter on the street simply
because Kierkegaard walked by. Kierkegaard, who was notoriously thin-skinned, never
put himself on a par with early Christian martyrs, yet he does describe himself as having endured a "martyrdom of laughter" at the hand of the *Corsair* (*Corsair Affair*, KW
13:236). Such a "martyrdom" was, in his eyes, sadly emblematic of his confused and
unserious age.

of Jesus in subsequent eras have any reason to expect a better fate. (As we have seen, he does not believe that there is ever such a thing as a "Christian society.") The more one is a true witness to Christ, the more Kierkegaard believes one risks becoming a martyr for him. Kierkegaard takes very seriously Jesus's command that "If any want to become my followers, let them deny themselves and take up their cross and follow me" (Matt 16:24). He is convinced that authentic Christians necessarily suffer in two ways: first, because they renounce their own pleasure and comfort for the sake of others; and second, because society (even a "Christian" society) punishes rather than rewards them for doing so.[28] We will return to the theme of suffering in Kierkegaard's work—and note potential dangers with it—at the end of this chapter.

All in all, the entirety of Kierkegaard's literary corpus consists in more than twenty published works, about half of which are signed in his own name and half of which are pseudonymous. He also left behind an even vaster quantity of journals and unpublished papers. As we saw at the beginning of this chapter, Kierkegaard's literary comet blazed with a particularly harsh glare during his "attack upon Christendom" in the last year of his life. Frustrated with his inability to renew his society through the subtleties of his prior writings, he ascended to ever greater heights of hyperbole by denouncing Lutheran clergy as frauds, swindlers, and cannibals.

Then his spent comet fell quickly from the sky. At the age of only forty-two, Kierkegaard collapsed in the street. He was taken to the hospital, where he remained until his death about six weeks later. During this time, his older brother Peter Christian, who was now a pastor in the Danish Lutheran church, visited the hospital in the hope of offering him Holy Communion. Kierkegaard said he would like to receive the sacrament, but only from a lay person, not a pastor—something the Danish church would never allow. So he died without receiving the sacrament. Hospital staff members were never able to determine the precise condition that ailed him. In a previous writing, Kierkegaard had instructed future eulogists to say simply that he died of a "longing for eternity."[29]

Kierkegaard did not want to be venerated as a saint or the originator of a new theology. He never called readers to imitate any of the specifics of his often-troubled life. He wanted only to spark in himself and his readers

---

28. See *Works of Love*, KW 16:194–96.

29. *Point of View*, KW 22:97.

a more passionate longing for eternity. His goal was to push himself and others one step farther down the path of "becoming a Christian."

Kierkegaard the Lutheran

Kierkegaard may be one of Lutheranism's strongest critics, yet his criticisms almost always radicalize rather than reject key themes of the Lutheran theological tradition. We have already noted Kierkegaard's rootedness in Lutheran theology when he affirms the subjective nature of faith. You have probably spotted a number of other characteristically Lutheran themes in the preceding discussion. Paradox, for example: Perhaps the only figure in the history of Christian thought to value paradox as highly as Kierkegaard as a defining feature of Christian truth is Martin Luther himself. Or the theology of the cross: Although Kierkegaard does not use this specific term, he shares Luther's conviction that God is revealed not in glory or power (or anything valued by human reason), but in the humble life and ignominious death of Jesus of Nazareth. We will see in this section that Kierkegaard often appropriates Lutheran themes so radically that they acquire a sharply subversive edge. We will also see that his Lutheran colors tend to show themselves most vividly precisely when he is denouncing Luther, Lutherans, and Lutheranism.[30]

Kierkegaard's Luther

Kierkegaard respects Martin Luther greatly and is certainly influenced by his theology, but he also refuses to glorify Luther and his theology as beyond reproach. He recognizes Luther's imperfections as a human being and feels free to criticize him when necessary. Still, he believes that the lion's share of the blame for the failings of Lutheranism belongs with later Lutherans, who parrot Luther's ideas without any of his passionate striving. Ultimately, Kierkegaard shows his fidelity to Luther less by repeating what he *said* than by doing what he *did*: challenging the social, ecclesial, and theological status quo in the name of Christ.

Kierkegaard sees a chasm between the self-satisfaction of Lutheran Christendom and Luther's own passionate efforts to follow Jesus. Indeed,

30. In many ways, this anticipates Dorothee Soelle's complex relationship to the Lutheran church that she, too, was born and baptized into, even if Soelle takes her theological bearings more directly from Dietrich Bonhoeffer. See chapter 4 below.

he writes with some irony that Luther is the rare case of a theologian whose "life is better than his preaching."[31] Lutherans often talk about Luther's *Anfechtungen* (or spiritual struggles) as tragic afflictions over which he triumphed. In contrast, Kierkegaard values these struggles as evidence of the earnestness of Luther's striving. From Kierkegaard's perspective, one of the fundamental problems with Lutheranism is that it wants to isolate Luther's teaching from the lived context in which he developed it. This "objectifies" Luther's reforming spirit, turning it into an ideology that merely validates the status quo. Kierkegaard believes that Luther's affirmation of salvation by grace alone only makes sense against the backdrop of his earnest efforts to live out God's commands. "[Luther's] life expressed works—let us never forget that," Kierkegaard writes. "But he said: A person is saved by faith alone."[32] From Kierkegaard's perspective, the message of Luther's life is at least as significant as that of his words. Each must be interpreted in light of the other.

Kierkegaard sometimes reminds his Lutheran readers of just how radical Luther's writings could be. In his journal, he contemplates memorizing one of Luther's sermons and preaching it verbatim from the pulpit as though it were his own. He is confident that the Lutherans around him would be furious—until he explained who really wrote the sermon.[33] At other times, Kierkegaard insists that, because the needs and deficiencies of his society are so different from those that Luther confronted, fidelity to Luther's vision requires presenting a very different message than he did. In fact, Kierkegaard believes that, in his context, "Luther's true successor will come to resemble the exact opposite of Luther." He argues that "Luther came after the preposterous overstatement of asceticism; whereas [the true successor] will come after the horrible fraud to which Luther's view gave birth."[34] Kierkegaard thus insists that Luther's own theology compels him to emphasize works far more than Luther did. To take just one example of this, Kierkegaard makes much of the Epistle of James—Luther's least favorite New Testament book, which he famously dismissed as "an epistle of straw."[35] Kierkegaard believes that if there is one biblical verse that his society needs to hear it is James's proclamation that "faith without works is

31. *JP* 3:2509 (1849), p. 78.

32. *For Self Examination*, KW 21:16.

33. *JP* 3:2493 (1849), p. 72–73.

34. *JP* 3:2518 (1850), p. 82.

35. *For Self Examination*, KW 21:13–25.

dead." He is confident that, if Luther lived in his world, he would be preaching this verse zealously as well.

Even though Kierkegaard often speaks of Luther admiringly, he also does not shy away from criticizing him. Kierkegaard worries that, especially late in his career, Luther became too worldly and comfortable, content to equate Christianity with "an optimism anticipating that we are to have an easy life in this world."[36] No one can doubt that the early years of Luther's career were marked by great personal struggle and danger. Yet Kierkegaard considers the fact that Luther was not actually killed as a martyr to be a black mark against him. He recoils from his mental picture of the late Luther as a beloved family man, sitting at his dinner table "in placid comfort, ringed by admiring adorers who believe that if he simply breaks wind it is a revelation or the result of inspiration."[37] This is not Kierkegaard's picture of a "truth-witness," to say the least. His dark vision is that "true reforming always makes life difficult, lays on burdens," such that "the true reformer is always slain."[38] Kierkegaard cannot help but see the numerous followers and friends that Luther gained as evidence that he had compromised the gospel. In his judgment, Luther lost sight of his own best insights about the subjective, individual, and counter-cultural nature of faith.

Radicalizing Luther: Law *and* Gospel

As we have seen, Kierkegaard's most radical criticisms of Luther and Lutheranism are almost always rooted in Lutheran themes. Perhaps the clearest example of this is Kierkegaard's critical embrace of the law/gospel paradigm, one of the characteristic motifs of Lutheran theology. Luther famously wrote that "whoever knows well how to distinguish the Gospel from the Law should give thanks to God and know that he is a real theologian."[39] Kierkegaard believes that among Lutherans this pattern has become so formulaic that it leads away from Christ rather than toward him. However, instead of jettisoning law and gospel, Kierkegaard carries this paradigm further than even Luther dared.

If you've sat through a few Lutheran sermons, you can probably recognize the law/gospel formula easily. The stereotypical Lutheran sermon

36. *JP* 3:2554 (1854), p. 103.

37. *JP* 3:2546 (1854), p. 98.

38. *JP* 3:2481 (1849), p. 69.

39. Luther, "Lectures on Galatians," *LW* 26:115.

begins with the preaching of "the law," the recitation of God's demands. Luther encourages preachers to present God's standard of righteousness in the most strenuous terms possible. For example, the preacher might remind listeners that not only does the fifth commandment forbid killing (something that most of us, thankfully, do not do on a regular basis), but also implicitly forbids hurting people in any way (a prohibition that most of us, sadly, violate routinely). Curiously, from a traditional Lutheran point of view, the primary purpose of the law is *not* to enable people to follow it. Luther taught that human beings are so sinful that they will *never* be able to follow God's commands, no matter how hard they try. The Lutheran view is that the function of the law is to show people their helplessness as sinners, their powerlessness to save themselves. In other words, the law is meant to prepare sinners to receive "the gospel," the good news that God saves by grace alone. Only after being humbled by their failure to achieve righteousness on their own can people truly open themselves to God's grace.

This rhetorical pattern is valuable in principle, but it is easy to see how it can become formulaic and trivial in practice. First, listeners are condemned for their failure to measure up to an impossible standard; then, their shame and terror piqued, they are reassured with the comfort of grace, the take-away conclusion of the sermon. All that unpleasantness about actually trying to follow God's commandments becomes a distant memory. With grace as my golden ticket, what need is there to actually change my life? Kierkegaard believes that such complacency is the characteristic failure of Lutheranism. The doctrine of grace becomes, in his words, a "fig leaf" used to hide Lutherans' failure even to *try* to imitate Jesus.[40] Anti-Climacus (a late pseudonym) writes in *Practice in Christianity* that according to this Lutheran mindset, "a universal discharge is given and assumed for all of us, a discharge all around," which proclaims that the Christian task is merely "to be an agreeable person just like the rest of us."[41] Kierkegaard's critique of this Lutheran failure serves as a key source of inspiration for the critique of "cheap grace" offered by Dietrich Bonhoeffer, the subject of the next chapter.

Given these criticisms, you might think that Kierkegaard would simply abandon the language of law and gospel altogether. Instead, he doubles down on it by interpreting law and gospel in quintessentially Lutheran terms as *paradox*, rather than a two-step rhetorical pattern. He argues that

40. *JP* 3:2481 (1849), p. 70.

41. *Practice in Christianity*, KW 20:215, 218.

preaching Christ requires speaking both law and gospel at once, with neither one allowed to trump the other. We are called to follow God's commands in every particular, *and* we are forgiven when we fail. Jesus loves each of us irrespective of our works, *and* trusting him means heeding his call to "follow me." Kierkegaard likes to use the similarity between the Danish words for "gift" (*Gave*) and "task" (*Opgave*) to signal that Christ is both of these at once, just as he is fully human and fully divine. He thus interprets many familiar words of Jesus as koan-like statements of paradox. For example, he interprets Jesus's words "Come to me" (Matt 11:28) as both the most gracious of invitations (since Jesus is the savior of the world) and the strictest of demands (since following him requires a lifetime of self-denial).[42] Similarly, he interprets the verse "one who is forgiven little loves little" (Luke 7:47) as "law" insofar as it condemns those who love little, but as "gospel" insofar as it suggests that love can increase through the experience of being forgiven.[43] How could law and gospel present us with anything other than paradox, Kierkegaard asks, if their source is Christ?

Always Reforming

Kierkegaard's most considered judgment of Luther is that he was a valuable and necessary "corrective" to Christianity at a particular moment, but not an absolute theological authority for all time. One might perhaps expect a Lutheran to accord greater stature to the founder of his theological movement. Yet the key to understanding Kierkegaard's judgment is that he does not believe that any theologian—including himself—can ever be more. Kierkegaard limits himself to the status of "corrective" every bit as much as he does Luther. He insists that no human being *ever* presents Christian truth in all-encompassing and timeless way. Because we always relate to Christ in the midst of particular circumstances, our vision of him will always be partial. No matter how hard we try, we are always bound to emphasize one side of the paradoxes of Christianity at the expense of the other. Just as Kierkegaard insists that he is not a Christian, so too he warns that he has no timeless doctrine to offer. He goes so far as to describe his voluminous authorship as nothing but "a little dash of cinnamon" that a cook adds to a dish.[44] The dish in this metaphor is the entirety of Christian truth, and the

42. *Christian Discourses*, KW 17:262–67.

43. *Without Authority*, KW 18:169–77.

44. *The Moment*, KW 23:422.

cook who oversees it is God. Kierkegaard's writings are but the "seasoning" or "correction" that God requires at a particular moment. Luther battles the excesses of late medieval asceticism and works righteousness; Kierkegaard protests the complacency of established Lutheranism. It is not that one is right and the other is wrong, but that God uses each of them to reform different shortcomings at different times.

Kierkegaard's insistence that Christian truth can never be encapsulated in a set of abstract doctrines is both faithful to Luther's best insights and valuable as a reminder to theology today. On this point, Kierkegaard echoes the Reformation principle *ecclesia semper reformanda est*: "a church is always to be reformed." He suggests that Christian theology, like Christian life, is always in process. Theology at its best is only ever *becoming* what God wants it to be. Born out of the need for reform, the Lutheran tradition should know this well. Yet it frequently loses sight of this truth. Kierkegaard teaches us to recognize that even our most cherished doctrines, prohibitions, and certainties may turn out to be in need of "seasoning" or "correction" as the circumstances in which we relate to Christ change.

Kierkegaard's own theology thus empowers us, as his readers, to recognize his limitations and to adapt his message to our own specific contexts. Indeed, if we are to be faithful to Kierkegaard's vision today, then I believe we must read him with the same critical and reforming eye that he brought to Luther's theology and that Luther brought to the church of his day.

Critiquing the Critic: Questions for Kierkegaard

Emboldened by Kierkegaard's affirmation of theology's never-ending need for reform, I now wish to highlight three sorts of critical questions that contemporary readers may wish to ask about his theology. Because the heart of Kierkegaard's project is to get you to think for yourself about what following Christ means, you should feel free to raise additional questions of your own.

1. *What is the value of Christian community?* Lutherans—certainly all the other Lutheran theologians in this book—tend to talk a lot about community. If you are reading this at a Lutheran college, then I'm sure you can vouch for this. At the same time, you may well question whether the reality of your college's community life really matches the promises peddled in its glossy brochures. Kierkegaard's prophetic voice empowers us to condemn the hypocrisy of individuals and institutions alike. At the same time, it is

legitimate to ask whether his writings are excessively negative in their critiques of the institutional church and unnecessarily closed to the potential value of Christian communities.

As we have seen, Kierkegaard envisions Christianity in highly individual terms. When he writes about the church, it is almost always to unmask its failures. Yet even if Kierkegaard is correct that no community is inherently "Christian," might communities of fellow strivers nonetheless provide a context or arena in which an individual's faith can grow? If faith consists in a lifetime of becoming in the image of Christ, might communities spur individuals along this path? *Fear and Trembling* makes much of the solitude of Abraham, but Abraham is far from the only biblical picture of faith. For example, the apostle Paul talks a good deal about faith communities—describing believers as constituting the "body of Christ" together and arguing that "if one member suffers, all suffer together with it" (1 Cor 12:27, 26). Paul celebrates the diversity within the body of Christ and encourages all within it to "bear one another's burdens" (Gal 6:2). Even at their best, Christian communities only ever live out this calling imperfectly. But to the extent that they do live it out, should we not affirm that they embody a Christian mission?

One of Kierkegaard's favorite Bible verses is Luke 6:44: "Each tree is known by its own fruit." He uses this verse as the centerpiece of the opening chapter of *Works of Love* to argue that, while the presence of love in a person's heart can never be objectively seen, it will inevitably make itself manifest in the world through loving actions. Might we not analyze the communities to which we belong in a similar way? I would argue that Kierkegaard's own best insights should challenge us to evaluate our congregations, small-group Bible studies, church-related colleges, and national church institutions "according to their fruit." This should lead us to pose questions such as the following: Does this community challenge me to be more attentive to the needy, vulnerable, and oppressed? Does it inspire me to seek peace in the world and in my personal relationships? Does it spur me to care for the earth? Does it encourage me to bring comfort and strength to people I might otherwise ignore? When the answer to these questions is No, we must work to reform our communities. But I do not think we should assume that the answer to these questions can never be Yes. After all, if Kierkegaard's writings succeed at least sometimes in challenging us as readers to love God more passionately and the people of this world more compassionately, then can we not hope to build communities that do the same?

2. *What does Christianity mean for society and the common good?* In the previous chapter, Samuel Torvend helped us to appreciate Luther's neglected vision of a just society that cares for the poor, provides healthcare to the sick, and educates all children well. At least on their face, Kierkegaardian ethics contrast sharply with this aspect of Luther's theology because they are so individualistic. His vision of what it means to follow in Jesus's footsteps is almost exclusively about the transformation of the individual rather than society. As we have seen, Kierkegaard rejects claims about societal progress and the value of group identity. Moreover, he can be remarkably calloused to economic and political injustices. He was a conservative royalist his entire life, and he was viscerally opposed to the very idea of democracy. In *Works of Love*, he states that Christianity is unconcerned with differences in earthly station (including wealth and poverty) and thus "will not abolish dissimilarity, neither the dissimilarity of distinction nor of lowliness."[45] Even though Kierkegaard shares a birthday with Karl Marx, who was just five years his junior, he has none of Marx's passion for revolutionizing society for the benefit of the oppressed.[46]

As readers of Kierkegaard today, we may well be persuaded by his conviction that no social order will ever amount to a utopia. Human efforts, it seems fair to say, will never bring about the kingdom of God on earth. Nonetheless, should this conviction stop us from striving to improve the society in which we live? Should the Kierkegaardian ideals of loving one's neighbor and imitating Christ not inspire us to reform societal patterns in addition to our own individual choices? After all, we, unlike Kierkegaard, *do* live in a democracy. Shouldn't our faith shape the laws and leaders and policies that we, as citizens, support and oppose? To take just one example among numerous social injustices in the contemporary United States, how can Christians ignore the fact that African Americans are incarcerated at nearly six times the rate of white Americans?[47] Is the ideal of Christian love really satisfied by merely eliminating racist thoughts from our own individual minds? Does the love of Jesus not call us to work to dismantle the societal structures that perpetuate this injustice and those like it?

45. *Woks of Love*, KW 16:88.

46. Dorothee Soelle, who does take much from Marx, will differ considerably here. See chapter 4 below.

47. "Criminal Justice."

3. *Lastly, should Christians seek suffering—or strive to alleviate it?* Reading this chapter, you have likely noted that Kierkegaard's vision of Christianity can sometimes be a very bleak one. Because he believes God to be revealed most fully in Jesus's suffering and death, Kierkegaard sees suffering (and even martyrdom) as characteristic of all true Christian lives. He believes that the result of following Jesus will almost certainly not be success, fame, wealth, or respect, but suffering. In my view, Kierkegaard is right to deny all versions of the prosperity gospel and to insist that truly following Jesus will always be a counter-cultural act. We need look no farther than the life of Dietrich Bonhoeffer (or Martin Luther King, Jr. or Oscar Romero or many other recent "truth witnesses") to see where working for God's justice can lead. Nonetheless, I resist Kierkegaard's assumption that suffering should be sought for its own sake—as though it were in and of itself a Christian goal.

Kierkegaard is not shy about presenting suffering as spiritually beneficial. He offers an entire series of meditations titled "The Gospel of Sufferings," which claim that "the school of suffering educates for eternity."[48] He argues that voluntary suffering is a surefire path to God because it encourages detachment from worldly things, trust in what is unseen, and unity with Christ, the great "suffering servant" and "man of sorrows." Kierkegaard goes so far as to say that "from the Christian point of view it is a plain duty to seek suffering in the same sense that from a purely human point of view it is a duty to seek pleasure."[49] Yet is this really true? Is suffering the goal of the Christian life—or its frequent, perhaps inevitable, byproduct? Should Christians seek suffering, or should they fight against it, even when doing so brings pain and persecution upon themselves? To put this point only slightly differently, did Jesus come to earth to suffer and die? Or did he come to *live* in a certain way—faithfully embodying God's love, justice, and nonviolence, even to the point of death?

As contemporary theologians have become more attentive to the multiple contexts in which Christianity is lived, they have rightly become increasingly critical of theologies of redemptive suffering such as Kierkegaard's. As we saw in the last section, Kierkegaard himself warns against universalizing a single theological perspective on what it means to follow Jesus. It may well be true that the call to join Jesus in suffering can be spiritually beneficial for someone who lives a life of security and privilege (as

48. *Upbuilding Discourses in Various Spirits*, KW 15:250.
49. *JP* 4:4631 (1849), p. 385.

Kierkegaard himself certainly did). But what would it mean to extol the spiritual benefits of suffering to a woman caught in an abusive relationship? Wouldn't this message perpetrate additional harm? Similarly, when white American preachers told slaves to "bear their cross" without complaining, so that their reward would be great in heaven, wasn't this an instrument of oppression? As recent theologians have argued, defining Christianity in terms of voluntary suffering not only ignores the experience of the disempowered but also perpetuates their victimization.

The subject of chapter four of this book, Dorothee Soelle, develops an alternative theology of suffering that is acutely sensitive to these concerns. As Jacqueline Bussie will show, Soelle is influenced by Luther's theology of the cross, but she takes this in a different direction than Kierkegaard does. She rejects all notions of suffering as redemptive or beneficial for the sufferer. At the same time, she affirms as a fundamental point of her theology that God is present not only in the cross of Jesus but also among all who suffer in our world—not because God values suffering, but because God wants to overcome it. This conviction affirms the absolute worth of everyone our world dismisses as "disposable." It calls would-be followers of Jesus to become allies and advocates for the oppressed, so that Jesus's words may be said of us: "For I was hungry and you gave me food, I was thirsty and you gave me something to drink, I was a stranger and you welcomed me, I was naked and you gave me clothing, I was sick and you took care of me, I was in prison and you visited me" (Matt 25:35–36). Each of these acts, it is important to recognize, is about alleviating suffering. Jesus asserts in this passage that it is in such acts—only in such acts, in fact—that his followers will see his face today.

That said, this Kierkegaardian warning still stands: walking this path is unlikely to win us the world's acclaim and may well bring us pain. As the recent water crisis in Flint, Michigan makes clear, even providing clean water to the vulnerable can be a contentious act. Individuals in Michigan who spoke out against the rising lead levels in the water were ostracized within the government and even lost their jobs. They were certainly not praised for defending access to clean water as a fundamental right. What the world rewards is cutting corners at the expense of the poor, not treating all people as beloved children of God. Nonetheless, however much we may suffer for giving water to the thirsty, is the ultimate goal of doing so not to bring health and wholeness to those in need, rather than to suffer for its own sake?

Conclusion

It is possible that the answers Kierkegaard would give to the questions I have raised above would not be to our liking. Yet he would be the first to remind us that he cannot answer them for us. If his theology teaches us anything, it is that we must do so for ourselves. Reflection, correction, seasoning, reformation—all of these are part of the never-ending journey of becoming a Christian as he conceives it. What false certainties tempt you and the Christians around you? In what ways are your life, your church, and your world in need of reform? What next step is Jesus's command to "follow me" calling you to take in your journey of becoming? Kierkegaard's writings will not answer these questions, but they will prod you to do so— *and to live that answer out.*

For Further Reading

Eller, Vernard. *Kierkegaard and Radical Discipleship: A New Perspective.* Princeton: Princeton University Press, 1968.

Garff, Joakim. *Søren Kierkegaard: A Biography.* Translated by Bruce H. Kirmmse. Princeton: Princeton University Press, 2005.

Hughes, Carl S. *Kierkegaard and the Staging of Desire: Rhetoric and Performance in a Theology of Eros.* New York: Fordham University Press, 2014.

Kierkegaard, Søren. *The Moment and Late Writings.* Translated by Howard V. Hong and Edna H. Hong. Princeton: Princeton University Press, 1989.

———. *Works of Love.* Translated by Howard V. Hong and Edna H. Hong. Princeton: Princeton University Press, 1995.

Kirkpatrick, Matthew D. *Attacks on Christendom in a World Come of Age: Kierkegaard, Bonhoeffer, and the Question of "Religionless Christianity."* Princeton Theological Monograph Series 166. Eugene, OR: Pickwick Publications, 2011.

Discussion Questions

1. How was Christianity, and especially "the Lutheran establishment," conventional and privileged in Kierkegaard's day? In what ways does it remain conventional and privileged today? Is this conventionality problematic? If so, what should a person—especially a would-be Christian—do about it?

2. In what ways does twenty-first-century America continue to equate faith with belief? How would Kierkegaard's description of faith as passionate and subjective (faith as more like love than objective knowledge) remain countercultural even today?

3. According to Hughes, Kierkegaard thought that the Lutheran law/gospel motif had become all-too formulaic in sixteenth-century Christendom. Do you also see problems with this? How might Christians best commend the work of discipleship without falling back into works-righteousness?

4. Which of Hughes's critical questions for Kierkegaard do you find most important? Why? What other critical questions would you pose to Kierkegaard?

3

Dietrich Bonhoeffer

Political Resistance in Tyrannical Times

Lori Brandt Hale

Early in the morning on April 9, 1945, German theologian and pastor Dietrich Bonhoeffer (1906–1945) was stripped naked, marched to the gallows, and executed by hanging at the Flossenbürg concentration camp.[1] He was considered an enemy of the state, an enemy of Nazi Germany, and those who killed him were rewarded with extra rations. Bonhoeffer's body was cremated, his ashes disposed of summarily, mixed with the ashes of other victims of the Third Reich, and no one from his family was notified. He was 39 years old.

Sin Boldly?

Dietrich Bonhoeffer *was* an enemy of the National Socialist (Nazi) state. He was a member of a conspiracy whose primary goal was to assassinate Adolf Hitler, the head of that state. By many measures, it was an odd role, and an unnecessary death, for a Lutheran theologian and pastor who had spent

1. Dietrich Bonhoeffer is one of the most important theologians of the twentieth century, with contributions that shape and will continue to shape our collective theological and ethical imaginations. Even though he was so young when he died, he wrote prolifically. His collected works, including books, papers, sermons, lectures, and letters, fill 16 volumes and have been collected and edited into English under the guidance of an editorial board. Known as the Dietrich Bonhoeffer Works—English Edition (DBWE), they make critical editions of all his work available to English speakers around the world.

much of his adult life committed to pacifism (or better: a peace ethic), who had planned to study nonviolent resistance with Gandhi, and who wrote extensively about loving one's enemies. But these were strange times. By Bonhoeffer's own account, he and his co-conspirators were living in a time and place in which "the huge masquerade of evil has thrown all ethical concepts into confusion" and in which evil appears in the "form of light, good deeds, historical necessity, [and] social justice . . ."[2] They were living in a time that required a radical form of ethical discernment, attuned to concrete reality and historical exigency.

That attention to concrete realities—especially in such *dark* times (that is, times that were both sinister and opaque, morally speaking)—served as the foundation for important theological themes that Bonhoeffer would develop, including redemptive solidarity with the most vulnerable, costly grace, and his profound notion of religionless Christianity. Many of these themes qualify Bonhoeffer as one of Luther's "theologians of the cross," those who join God in solidarity with those who suffer, and make difficult, countercultural decisions, especially in times where evil is disguised as good.[3] But Bonhoeffer, better than any other historical figure, also lives out another Lutheran theme. Luther wrote to his co-reformer Philip Melanchthon and famously (or infamously) advised him to "sin boldly, but believe and rejoice in Christ even more boldly."[4] Bonhoeffer echoes that very idea when, in early 1943, he gives an account of his decade-long resistance to Hitler and Nazism.

Bonhoeffer's account, in the form of a now famous essay of moral support and guidance for his co-conspirators and friends, marks ten years of their collective opposition, and finally resistance, to Hitler. In it, Bonhoeffer reflects on the difficulty of their charge. What does it mean—in the midst of the tumultuous, horrific, and confusing "masquerade of evil" known as Nazi Germany—to respond to the question and call of God, i.e. to act boldly? While most would assume that the resistance movement's civil disobedience, counterintelligence, and assassination plots were unambiguously

2. Bonhoeffer, "An Account at the Turn of the Year 1942–1943," in *Letters and Papers from Prison*, DBWE 8:38.

3. Recall that Luther's Heidelberg Disputation holds up "theologians of the cross" (those who find God fully revealed in suffering and the cross of Jesus) over-and-against "theologians of glory" (those who project onto God human aspirations and thus end up calling "evil good and good evil"). Luther, "Heidelberg Disputation," *LW* 31:52–53 (theses 19–21).

4. Luther, "To Philip Melanchthon," *LW* 48:282.

good, ethically or religiously speaking, Bonhoeffer suspects that any faith in their *rightness* might actually displace their faith in God. He writes, "Who stands firm? Only the one whose ultimate standard is not his reason, his principles, conscience, freedom, or virtue; only the one who is prepared to sacrifice all of these when, in faith and in relationship to God alone, he is called to obedient and responsible action."[5]

For Bonhoeffer, the Christian way of life is not first of all about "moral precepts," about right versus wrong, or even about virtue over vice. In fact, any such moral or theological clarity seems only to invite self-justification. But, because God through Christ radically frees Christians for responsible action in the world, such actions can be bold—indeed they may even be "sinful." In other words, Bonhoeffer never claims that it is morally acceptable to kill someone, even a tyrant. He does not try to morally justify the actions or intentions of the members of the conspiracy. He is convinced, in fact, that murder is sinful. Yet he is also convinced that sinful action—such as killing Adolf Hitler—can be the responsible and *Christian* thing to do, but it depends on taking the Gospel message of forgiveness seriously. It is this bold interpretation of God's radically good news that shapes Bonhoeffer's political vocation. Responding to it, he becomes both a Lutheran radical, willing to sacrifice his life for others, and a radical Lutheran, wholly dependent on a profound (and Lutheran) understanding of grace. Such grace makes space for that bold but responsible action to be sinful, enlivening Luther's "sin boldly, but believe and rejoice in Christ even more boldly."

Journey to Radical Sensibilities

Bonhoeffer's personal and theological journey to political resistance was made possible by the development of sensibilities best described as radical. It is a journey marked by many factors: personal tragedy, academic training, life-changing experiences and friendships, and the harsh realities of his historical time and place. His journey started when he was eleven years old, during World War I, with the death of a brother. It continued with his theological training, particularly at the University of Berlin, under the tutelage of three Lutheran scholars. It was shaped profoundly by an academic year at Union Theological Seminary in New York. It was sealed by Adolf Hitler's rise to power and his swift and alarming actions against Jews.

5. Bonhoeffer, "An Account," DBWE 8:40.

Which Calling?

Dietrich Bonhoeffer was born in Breslau, Germany on February 4, 1906 to Karl and Paula Bonhoeffer; he was the sixth of eight children. They were a well-educated, upper-middle-class family, politically active, but only nominally religious (in other words, they didn't go to church very often). Karl Bonhoeffer was a well-known professor of psychology and neurology, and Paula Bonhoeffer had a university degree at a time when most women of her age did not.

In 1917, when Dietrich and his twin sister, Sabine, were 11 years old, two of their older brothers, Karl-Friedrich and Walter, were called to serve in the German military in World War I. Within two weeks of leaving home, Walter was killed. His death had a profound impact on the whole family, including young Dietrich, who received Walter's confirmation Bible and began contemplating questions about life and death. He and Sabine discussed existential questions late at night, and the seeds of interest in pursuing the study of theology began to take root. When Bonhoeffer, at age 13, announced his plans to do just that—study theology—it came as a shock to his family. He was a very accomplished pianist, playing Mozart by the time he was ten; many thought he would pursue a vocation in music. His parents and siblings worried that he was taking an easy path or, worse, a boring one. But his father, realizing he had taught his children to be independent thinkers, was supportive.

Driven and brilliant, Dietrich finished his doctoral work by the time he was 21 years old, writing a dissertation titled, *Sanctorum Communio*, which means "the communion of saints." The dissertation explores what can be called the "sociality of theology," or the social intent of all Christian concepts. Even the most basic of questions in theological inquiry—for example, what does it mean to be human?—has an inherently social answer: human beings exist only in relationship to and responsibility for other human beings.[6]

Related was Bonhoeffer's idea of "Christ existing as community." It is both a complicated and a simple idea. The church community, he claims, is the place of the ongoing incarnation or embodiment of Christ. If Christians understand that God revealed Godself to the world through the Incarnation of Jesus of Nazareth—and they do—Bonhoeffer wondered about

---

6. Compare this emphasis on Christian community with Kierkegaard's attention to the "single individual," as explored in chapter 2 above.

the ongoing incarnation or the ongoing revelation of God in the world. Through his sociological and theological study of the church, he concluded that an ongoing incarnation happens in community. We see Christ in the other and present Christ to the other. Bonhoeffer's work underscores the importance of the sociality of theology, the centrality of Christ both in the church and in our relationships, and the integrity (or dignity) of all others as Other, as revealing God.[7] In fact, when we encounter another person, we are called into ethical relationship with and obligation to the Other through the mediation of Christ.

Two Kingdoms or Unity of Reality?

In 1930, Bonhoeffer received a Sloane Fellowship to study at Union Theological Seminary in New York City for the 1930–1931 academic year. He studied with Reinhold Niebuhr, often noted as the father of modern social ethics. Knowing the coming political activism that both shapes Bonhoeffer's life and causes his death, one might assume that he embraced his studies with Niebuhr and agreed, without hesitation, that one should preach with the Bible in one hand and the newspaper in the other. But that was not the case. Bonhoeffer was quite resistant to Niebuhr and disappointed with the academic rigor at Union.

Bonhoeffer's resistance to his coursework was rooted deeply in his Lutheran heritage. He was steeped in the Lutheran "doctrine" of two kingdoms; he embraced the idea that the worldly realm and the spiritual realm, while related, were indeed separate, with separate concerns, tasks, and sources of authority. Niebuhr and others challenged this idea.[8] With prompting by Niebuhr, Bonhoeffer re-examined Luther's original understanding of the relation between the sacred and secular and came to acknowledge a more intimate connection, a "unity of reality."

---

7. For an accessible, but more sustained, discussion of Bonhoeffer's idea of "Christ existing as community" as well as his understanding of the "other," see chapter 2 of Haynes and Hale, *Bonhoeffer for Armchair Theologians*. Other thinkers who address these questions include the Jewish philosophers, Buber, *I and Thou*; and Levinas, *Totality and Infinity*.

8. It is worth noting that Luther did not intend for the two kingdoms to be divided against each other, nor did he want the distinction to be used as an excuse for the church to be apathetic and inactive in the face of problems in the world. But that separation had been exaggerated over the years, and would be used by the Nazis to justify their encouragement of the church to stay out of state affairs.

Other relationships helped form and deepen this understanding as well. Jean Lassere was a young French student who would become active in the French Resistance during World War II and with whom Bonhoeffer became very close friends. They frequently cooked meals together and even took a road trip to Mexico. Lassere's strong commitment to pacifism shaped—or re-shaped—Bonhoeffer's thinking about many things, including the peace commandments of Jesus. Lassere also suggested a new way to read the Sermon on the Mount, Jesus's central discourse as recorded in Matthew's gospel (with parallels in Luke) that include "hard sayings" such as "do not resist an evildoer" (Matt 5:39), and "love your enemies and pray for those who persecute you" (5:44). Bonhoeffer had read the Sermon on the Mount and the Beatitudes in line with the Lutheran theological tradition, especially Luther's second, or "theological," use of the law. He thought they served to remind people about their shortcomings, their sinfulness. We could never possibly live up to the expectations set out in that sermon, so we must recognize our sinful nature and rely on God's grace for our salvation. Or, we must accept the idea that the ideals in the Beatitudes are intended for the kingdom of God and will be realized at the end of time. Lassere had a different sensibility. What if God intended Jesus's proclamations in the Sermon on the Mount as statements about how we are supposed to live our lives now, in this time and place? What if, Lassere wondered, the Sermon on the Mount was not a reminder of our fallen nature, but a mandate for living? This new idea was foundational for Bonhoeffer's later thinking that is both inherently Christological and devoted to seeing the world from the perspective of below, from the perspective of those who suffer.[9]

Another key friendship Bonhoeffer developed while at Union Theological Seminary was with Franklin Fisher, an African-American student from Alabama. Previously, Bonhoeffer had known few people of color in his life, and through this relationship with Fisher, Bonhoeffer witnessed and experienced the overwhelming racism of 1930s America. Bonhoeffer, Fisher, and some others went together to a restaurant where Fisher was

9. Bonhoeffer famously refers to Lassere in a letter he penned to Eberhard Bethge on July 21, 1944, from Tegel Prison: "I remember a conversation I had thirteen years ago with a young French pastor. We had simply asked ourselves what we really wanted to do with our lives. And he said, I want to become a saint (—and I think it's possible that he did become one). This impressed me very much at the time. Nevertheless, I disagreed with him, saying something like: I want to learn to have faith. For a long time I did not understand the depth of this antithesis." Bonhoeffer, *Letters and Papers from Prison*, DBWE 8:485.

refused service. Bonhoeffer was disgusted and led the dinner party out of the establishment in protest. The irony that he himself was a German national (an enemy) was not lost on Bonhoeffer. In a letter to his brother, Bonhoeffer wrote that he thought the racial divide was the biggest challenge the American church would face in the twentieth century.[10] He added that he saw nothing analogous in Germany to the racial bigotry he was witnessing in the United States. Just two years later, he would recognize that the Jews in Germany not only were in a similar situation to the African-Americans, but also were in much more imminent danger.

It is without question that Bonhoeffer's friendship with Frank Fisher fostered a sensitivity to racial discrimination and allowed him to see the danger for Jews in Germany under Nazi rule much earlier and much more clearly than most of his counterparts at the time. But their friendship is only part of this story. Fisher also introduced Bonhoeffer to the Abyssinian Baptist Church in Harlem. It was a spirit-filled African-American church with a visceral, call-and-response worship setting and hand-clapping gospel music. Bonhoeffer had never experienced anything like it. The classically trained pianist fell in love with the music and messages of the spirituals (and took recordings back to Germany). Partly through this music, he experienced the collapse of the division between the two kingdoms, of the earthly and the spiritual, or the secular and the sacred. Moreover, the "unity of reality" took further hold as this politically and socially conscious community, led by the dynamic and powerful Pastor Adam Clayton Powell, understood the connection between faith and action, or theology and activism. Flying banners outside the church that brought harsh truths about the world to light—for example, "A Man Was Lynched Today"—reinforced the idea that there are not, in fact, two kingdoms, but a single reality in which one lives out one's faith in relationship in and for others.

This Worldliness?

Through his encounters with Neibuhr, Lassere, Fisher and others, Bonhoeffer slowly but surely began to replace his traditional, Lutheran understanding of God's "two kingdoms" with a new understanding of the unity of reality. At the same time, he began to develop the related idea of a "this-worldly Christianity," one that was formed, in part, by his intellectual

10. This challenge has not lessened in the twenty-first century. See Wallis, *America's Original Sin.*

grappling with Lassere's ideas. In his *Ethics*, published posthumously, but written in the early 1940s, Bonhoeffer writes: "There are not two realities, but *only one reality*, and that is God's reality revealed in Christ in the reality of the world. Partaking in Christ we stand at the same time in the reality of God and in the reality of the world."[11] This one reality, inherently Christological in Bonhoeffer's understanding, and which took root in New York ten years earlier, is closer to Luther's original thinking than traditional Lutheran receptions of Luther on this matter. Moreover, the idea is sacramental and incarnational in a way that aligns with Luther's own thinking about Christ's presence in the sacraments. Luther writes,

> Wherever you place God for me, you must also place the humanity for me. They simply will not let themselves be separated and divided from each other. [Christ] has become one person and does not separate the humanity from himself as Master Jack takes off his coat and lays it aside when he goes to bed.[12]

Bonhoeffer's understanding of the unity of reality and the this-worldliness of Christianity largely follows suit—although he will radicalize these ideas according to pressing political concerns, as we shall soon see. What is more, it is evident that Bonhoeffer's affinity with Luther's theology of the cross is not coincidental. In a letter to Eberhard Bethge from Tegel Prison, Bonhoeffer writes:

> In the last few years I have come to know and understand more and more the profound this-worldliness of Christianity. The Christian is not a *homo religiosus* [religious person] but simply a human being, in the same way that Jesus was a human being—in contrast, perhaps, to John the Baptist. I do not mean the shallow and banal this-worldliness of the enlightened, the bustling, the comfortable, or the lascivious, but the profound this-worldliness that shows discipline and includes the ever-present knowledge of death and resurrection. I think Luther lived in this kind of this-worldliness.[13]

Bonhoeffer's sojourn in New York City, especially in Harlem as a congregant and a Sunday School teacher, embedded a sensibility in him that began to move the theological exploration of "Christ existing as community" of his doctoral work in a more concrete direction. A few years after his fellowship

11. Bonhoeffer, *Ethics*, DBWE 6:58.

12. Luther, "Confession Concerning Christ's Supper," *BTW*, 267.

13. Bonhoeffer, *Letters and Papers from Prison*, DBWE 8:485.

at Union Theological Seminary, Bonhoeffer was back in Berlin at the University. He played the recordings of Negro spirituals that he had acquired while worshipping at Abyssinian. One of his students reported Bonhoeffer saying, "When I took leave of my black friend, he said to me: 'Make our sufferings known in Germany, tell them what is happening to us and show them what we are like.' I wanted to fulfill this obligation tonight."[14] Bonhoeffer was already working to understand the place and suffering of Christ in the world, amongst us as well as to understand "this-worldliness" in a Lutheran kind of way. And he would continue to do so for the rest of his life.

Journey to Radical Action

Bonhoeffer's journey to radical sensibilities and, ultimately, radical action, was hastened by the election of Adolf Hitler. On January 30, 1933, Hitler became chancellor of the German Republic, which was financially and emotionally crippled by the consequences of the post-World War I Versailles Treaty and the failed attempts of the Weimar Republic to address these problems. Hitler promised to put people back to work, and he did. He broke the terms of the treaty, re-opened military manufacturing, re-invigorated a sense of national pride, and named a collective scapegoat: the Jews. The German people were ecstatic. Dietrich Bonhoeffer was not.[15] His academic training coupled with his year at Union had sharpened and radicalized his sensibilities.

As Hitler began to systematically isolate and dehumanize the Jews, Bonhoeffer was paying attention. As Hitler ordered a national boycott of Jewish businesses on April 1, 1933, Bonhoeffer was paying attention. As Hitler continued to lift up the Jews as the source of Germany's financial distress as well as limit their freedoms, Bonhoeffer took action. In April of 1933, Bonhoeffer delivered a stinging address to a group of pastors titled, "The Church and the Jewish Question." The essay does contain some problematic views about the relationship between Jews and Christians; namely,

---

14. Burton, "The Life of Dietrich Bonhoeffer," 29.

15. On February 1, 1933, just two days after Hitler took power, Bonhoeffer delivered a radio address titled, "The Younger Generation's Altered View of the Concept of the *Führer*," warning the listeners about a leader (*Führer*) who becomes a misleader (*Verführer*). His address was cut short, but his ability to see the dangers of the Nazi regime so clearly and so early was quite evident.

it espouses Christian supersessionism, the idea that Christianity has super-seded Judaism and that Jews/Israel must convert to Christ.[16] It is a position Bonhoeffer, later in his life, regrets holding. Nevertheless, the essay raised important questions about how the church should respond to state actions against the Jews and, more radically, called for the church to fight gross, political injustice. He made three unprecedented points that, again, flew in the face of the distorted doctrine of two kingdoms requiring a strong division between church and state. First, Bonhoeffer asserts that in a unified reality, the church must question the state and determine if it is providing too much or too little aid to its citizens; it must call the state to act responsibly. Second, the church has the right and responsibility to help victims of the state regardless of their religious identity or membership in the church. Finally, and most radically, the church must jam the spokes of the wheel of the state. In other words, Bonhoeffer was calling for direct political action led by the church!

Study with Gandhi or Lead an Illegal Seminary?

Bonhoeffer's heightened sensibilities prompted his prophetic call to the church, a radical action in itself. But his journey to radical conspiratorial action could have taken a different route. While serving two German-speaking churches in London in 1934—sorting out his role in resisting the National Socialists—Bonhoeffer made arrangements to visit and study with Gandhi in India. He was interested in learning more about nonviolent resistance and standing up to the Nazis in this way. His friend and colleague, Bishop George Bell, wrote a letter of introduction and Bonhoeffer passed a "fit to the live in the tropics" test. An invitation to go was his for the taking. It is interesting to consider what turns Bonhoeffer's life and work might have taken had he been able to follow this path. However, the newly formed

---

16. Supersessionism is the idea that the Christian faith, as newer and more complete, surpasses and supplants the religion of Judaism. Soulen, *The God of Israel*, 1–12; Wyschogrod, *Abraham's Promise*, 183–84. In this case it is largely synonymous with anti-Judaism, a theological position by which "the Jew" provides the negative other for Christian self-understanding, but should be distinguished from anti-Semitism, a racist ideology that first emerges in the fifteenth century and climaxes in National Socialism's pseudoscience. For connections between the two, see Carroll, *Constantine's Sword*. For a generous assessment from a Jewish point of view of Bonhoeffer's supersessionistic (anti-Jewish) theology, and how it nonetheless provided the grounds for its own overcoming and his political resistance, see Rubenstein, "Was Dietrich Bonhoeffer a Righteous Gentile?"

Confessing Church, founded in protest to the Nazi-led *Reich* Church (or state church, also known as the German Christians), needed someone to train new pastors.

Confessing Church leaders invited Bonhoeffer to come lead the illegal and underground seminary, and he said yes. As much as he wanted to go to India, he recognized that he was needed to prepare new pastors for the difficult task of leading and preserving churches in the context of Nazi Germany. The seminary, located at Finkenwalde, was supported by local Confessing Church congregations as well as nearby landowners, and Bonhoeffer himself. Bonhoeffer's personal library became the seminary's library. Congregations donated furniture and household items. Sustained financial support came from people like Ruth von Kleist-Retzow, whose granddaughter, Maria, would later become Bonhoeffer's fiancé. For years, he had been speculating about the nature of community, about Christ existing as community. This offer was a chance to put his ideas into practice.

Bonhoeffer's approach to running the seminary was experimental. He sought to create a strong communal sensibility by providing the students with a highly structured experience. There was time together and time alone, time to pray, work, worship, and play. Some accused Bonhoeffer of trying to "monasticize" the seminarians. But he was undeterred, and determined to offer training that would embolden the young men as they stepped up to shepherd congregations in the throes of a destructive nationalism. Even while immersed in their studies, the seminarians were prompted by Bonhoeffer to discuss political realities, to understand church-state relations, and to consider refusing military conscription, if called. These discussions became forms of radical action and Bonhoeffer became known and labeled as a pacifist and enemy of the state.

Cheap Grace or Costly Grace?

While Bonhoeffer was serving as the seminary director, he was thinking and writing about what he calls "costly grace." In fact, one of the ideas for which he is most famously known is his conviction that grace is costly. He wrote about it in his book *Nachfolge* (translated as *Discipleship*), published in 1937.[17] *Nachfolge* literally means "following after." For Bonhoeffer, fol-

---

17. The first English translation sought to capture the importance of Bonhoeffer's ideas by titling the book, *The Cost of Discipleship*, but the new DBWE edition of *Discipleship* offers a more direct translation of the German title, *Nachfolge*.

lowing after turns out to be a very costly affair. His choice to follow after—to suffer redemptively on behalf of others just as Christ suffered redemptively on behalf of the whole of humanity—marked his commitment to faith and obedience, even unto death. His willingness to take radical political action cost him his life.

Bonhoeffer's distinction between "cheap grace" and "costly grace" is more than a call to sacrificial action. It is a theological insight related to his understanding of Luther's doctrine of justification. In brief, justification is about "getting right" with God. Anyone who has ever typed a document on a computer has thought about justification in this simple sense. If you select "left justify," the words are aligned on the left side of the page. "Right justify" lines up the words on the right side of the page. "Both justify" aligns the words with the margins on both sides of the paper (as with the text on this page). Christians want to be "lined up" with, or justified, in the eyes of God.

Even though justification is a relatively simple theological concept, it leads to central disagreements between Christians. To appreciate Bonhoeffer's understanding of justification, it is necessary to consider two key historical interpretations of the term: the classical Protestant doctrine articulated by Martin Luther and the traditional Catholic position formulated by Augustine.[18] Augustine and Luther agree that justification is possible only through God's gift of grace. They differ, however, on the nature of that gift.

For Augustine, God's grace is a gift that transforms the recipient's thinking, willing, and believing so that he or she can love what God loves. The sinner, in Augustine's view, suffers from disordered loves; God's transformative gift of grace enables each person to reorder those loves and make God one's primary concern. God's forgiveness follows, but only in accord with one's own penitent and righteous actions.[19]

For Martin Luther, on the other hand, God's grace is a gift given in response to one's declaration or affirmation of faith. As Samuel Torvend recounts above, Martin Luther—as a young Augustinian monk—struggled with the concept of justification. In particular, he wrestled with a verse in

18. These two doctrines of justification are also known as the "declarative" doctrine and the "transformative" doctrine.

19. Augustine's biography sheds light on his interpretation of justification. His conversion to Christianity came late in his life, after a series of questionable choices. He needed to change the way he was willing, thinking, believing, and acting. See Augustine, *Confessions*.

Paul's letter to the Romans that reads, "The one who is righteous will live by faith" (Rom 1:17). Luther thought he had to be righteous before he could live by faith. To that end, he went to confession every day. Later, Luther came to understand righteousness—or justification—as a gift of unconditional mercy and forgiveness. In Luther's mature view, sinful humans could never do enough or be enough to line themselves up with God. So Paul's assertion in Romans that "the one who is righteous will live by faith" describes righteousness as a generous gift from God. Accepting that gift, that grace, requires only that one declares one's faith; hence the famous Lutheran dictum: justification through grace by faith alone.

There are adherents and critics on both sides of this debate. On one hand, those who are critical of Luther's interpretation of justification say it produces lazy Christians. If God's grace is sheer mercy, why do anything good at all? On the other hand, opponents of the traditionally Catholic or Augustinian interpretation of justification fear that Christians must "earn" their salvation through "works righteousness."

Bonhoeffer acknowledges the potential of the Lutheran position to encourage lazy, even apathetic, Christians. Lutherans and other Protestant Christians who do not recognize with James that faith without works is dead embrace what Bonhoeffer calls "cheap grace." Bonhoeffer emphasizes that while the proclamation of grace (or the "declarative" doctrine of justification) affirms the unconditional mercy of God's grace, it encourages, even requires, transformation as well. In fact, Bonhoeffer asserts that those who think grace does not require discipleship misunderstand Luther.

Without abandoning Luther's basic affirmation that justification comes by faith alone, Bonhoeffer calls for an acknowledgment that grace—even and especially "free" grace—is costly: "Costly grace . . . comes to us as a gracious call to follow Jesus; it comes as a forgiving word to the fearful spirit and the broken heart. Grace is costly, because it forces people under the yoke of following Jesus Christ; it is grace when Jesus says: 'My yoke is easy and my burden is light' (Matt 11:30)."[20] With his notion of "costly grace," Bonhoeffer reasserts Luther's understanding of the link between grace and discipleship, while establishing a middle ground between the two classical versions of justification.[21] For him, the crucial distinction between cheap

---

20. Bonhoeffer, *Discipleship*, DBWE 4:45.

21. It is a middle ground that anticipates the Joint Declaration of the Doctrine of Justification issued by the World Lutheran Federation and the Roman Catholic Church in 1999.

and costly grace lies in the fact that costly grace acknowledges the correlation of grace and discipleship, while cheap grace misses it altogether. Cheap grace is "the preaching of forgiveness without repentance . . . [it is] the Lord's Supper without confession of sin; it is absolution without personal confession."[22] Bonhoeffer continues, it "is grace without discipleship, grace without the cross, grace without the living, incarnate Jesus Christ."[23] Bonhoeffer goes so far as to say that cheap grace is the mortal enemy of the church: "Like ravens we have gathered around the carcass of cheap grace. From it we have imbibed the poison which has killed the following of Jesus among us."[24]

Life under cheap grace, Bonhoeffer claims, does not differ from life under sin. There is no following after Christ because cheap grace justifies the sin without transforming the sinner. Bonhoeffer cannot emphasize strongly enough the unbreakable link between God's generous gift of grace and God's call to "follow after." Justification is a gift of grace, but it is not a gift that renders Christians free from responsibility. On the contrary, freedom from sin through (costly) grace makes it possible to follow Christ. In a way that prefigures the claims he will make in *Letters and Papers from Prison* about living a "this-worldly" life, Bonhoeffer reaffirms Luther's own appropriation of the doctrine of justification:

> Luther's reason for leaving the monastery was not the justification
> of sin, but justification of the sinner. Costly grace was given as a
> gift to Luther. It was grace, because it was water onto thirsty land,
> comfort for anxiety, liberation from the servitude of a self-chosen
> path, forgiveness of all sins. The grace is costly, because it did not
> excuse one from works. Instead, it endlessly sharpened the call to
> discipleship.[25]

Those who level the harshest critique against Luther's doctrine of justification, Bonhoeffer would argue, are those who least understand it. They fail to recognize that, for Luther, *God's gracious gift of forgiveness meant that one must understand the call to discipleship more deeply and seriously than ever.* In Bonhoeffer's terms, the call to discipleship was a call to responsible

22. Bonhoeffer, *Discipleship*, DBWE 4:55.

23. Ibid., 44.

24. Ibid., 53.

25. Ibid., 49. Compare Kierkegaard's parallel quest to reconnect Luther's "doctrine" of grace to Luther's own passionate strivings, as described by Hughes in chapter 2 above.

action, and in the context of Nazi Germany, responsible action required direct political resistance.

Breaking the Law to Follow Jesus?

In 1937, the Gestapo locked the seminary doors in Finkenwalde. The experiment in community was over; the seminary was dissolved. Bonhoeffer set up "collective pastorates" for his remaining students; they were apprenticed to clergy serving in established, and legal (although now compromised) Confessing Churches. The overwhelming concern for Confessing Church leaders was whether to sign a loyalty oath to Hitler. There was disagreement among church leaders; some supported signing under certain circumstances. Bonhoeffer was displeased with the lines of rupture this divided approach was causing. At the same time, his own family remained focused on other concerns. Bonhoeffer's twin sister, Sabine, was married to Gerhard Leibholz, a "non-Aryan." Even though he was a Christian, his father was Jewish. By the fall of 1938, it became evident that it was no longer safe for them to stay in Germany, so they made the agonizing decision to leave the country.

Within months of their departure, the horrors facing all the Jews under the Nazis were made exceptionally clear. On November 9, 1938, Jewish synagogues, homes, and businesses throughout Germany were vandalized and burned. Known as *Krystallnacht*, or the Night of Broken Glass, many scholars mark this night as a turning point for Bonhoeffer. Before *Krystallnacht*, Bonhoeffer wrote and preached about "loving one's enemies"; after *Krystallnacht*, he wrote about "responsible action." Before *Krystallnacht*, he was involved in the church struggle and worried about the negative and destructive impact of National Socialism on the churches. After *Krystallnacht*, he joined a political conspiracy and worried about the devastating and deadly impact the Nazis were having on the whole world. Undoubtedly, the events of that awful night and the silence of the churches in its aftermath, including the silence of the Confessing Church, were key steps on his journey to radical action.

In late 1938, renewed calls for Bonhoeffer's conscription into the German army prompted him to consider leaving Germany. With an invitation from Reinhold Niebuhr to return to the United States, Bonhoeffer sailed for America on June 2, 1939. Immediately upon his arrival, however, he felt as if he had made an error in judgment.[26] Friends and colleagues tried to persuade Bonhoeffer to stay in New York in safety, but on July 8 he boarded the last ship to make the Atlantic crossing before it was closed. Bonhoeffer returned to Germany. He had a sense, even if the details were not yet clear, that to return to Germany would require a dangerous obedience to God. With strong family ties to the *Abwehr*, the German Military Intelligence Agency and the center of anti-Hitler resistance, that obedience led him to his involvement in the conspiracy, a radical action indeed.

Journey to a Radical Theology of the Cross

The experiences, historical contexts, and Lutheran ideas that shaped Dietrich Bonhoeffer's radical sensibilities and actions are the same ones that fueled his theological imagination and shaped his radical theology. More specifically, Bonhoeffer's radical theology is predicated on a profound awareness of suffering in the world and a ubiquitous Lutheran theology of the cross. The theological ideas that Bonhoeffer wrote about in the last few years of his life, including acting on behalf of others in the world, taking responsible and ethical action, and recognizing the sometimes hidden place of God in the world, cannot be disconnected from his deep embrace of Luther's theology of the cross.

Should I Act on Behalf of Others?

The first of those ideas is a pivotal concept in Bonhoeffer's work from his dissertation to the letters and papers written in prison, but he doesn't name it until he starts writing his *Ethics*. Finally, he captures the idea in the German word *Stellvertretung*, which means, "vicarious representative action." Vicarious means "to act in the place of," which is one way to talk about Christ's suffering and death on the cross. *Stellvertretung* is Bonhoeffer's description of how human beings are to be in the world. Christ lived and died vicariously for all humanity. Likewise, those who follow after Christ, his disciples, are called to vicarious action and responsible love on behalf of others, especially those who suffer. This idea is the precursor to Bonhoeffer's

---

26. "I have made a mistake in coming to America. I must live through this difficult period of our national history with the Christian people of Germany. I will have no right to participate in the reconstruction of Christian life in Germany after the war if I do not share the trials of this time with my people." Bethge, *Dietrich Bonhoeffer*, 655.

radical notion that it is best to see the events of the world from the perspective of those who suffer; he calls it "the view from below."[27]

To be clear, the concept of *Stellvertretung* has a moral component in addition to a theological one. It is not limited to the work of a Christian in the church community but refers to a way of being and acting in the world applicable to all people—a way that defines one's humanity. In a beautiful twist on the classical theological dictum that God became human so that humans might become divine, Bonhoeffer argues that God became human so that humans could become *truly human*. Perhaps it goes without saying, but this turn of the classical phrase is rooted in Bonhoeffer's clear appropriation of Luther's theology of the cross—that is, the conviction that the fullness of God is revealed in the humanity of Jesus, especially in his suffering and death. It also makes it possible to understand Bonhoeffer's affirmation, in agreement with Luther, that the freedom which comes by way of the cross is not a *freedom from* but a *freedom to*. It is not freedom from responsibility nor is it a freedom from rules that gives license to act on one's every whim. Rather, the freedom which comes by way of the cross is freedom to serve the neighbor and the world; it is the freedom to be not only more human, but more humane.

This Christ-centered view of freedom as suffering service is at the very heart of Bonhoeffer's ethics. In Bonhoeffer's case, service to the neighbor took the form of protecting his Jewish neighbors from suffering and dying in concentration camps. But to do so required taking on guilt. That is, to act on behalf of victims of the Nazi state required duplicity, treason, and murder. It required sin. Remember Luther's charge to Melancthon? "Sin boldly." Bonhoeffer was willing, in obedience to the call of God, to sin boldly on behalf of those who could not act for themselves. But, just as Luther's bold claim depends on the saving Christ ("Sin boldly, but believe and rejoice in Christ even more boldly"), Bonhoeffer recognized that such sinful action was made possible only by the grace and forgiveness that comes through Christ's vicarious act. He is wholly dependent on that generous gift of grace. The *freedom to* take on guilt, on behalf of others, is radical action made possible by radical theology.

27. Bonhoeffer, "An Account," DBWE 8:52.

What Is Responsible Christian Action in the World?

By 1940, Bonhoeffer had begun his work as a double agent for the *Abwehr*. Ostensibly, he was using his ecumenical contacts throughout Europe to gather intelligence for Germany. In reality, he was making those contacts, but trying to negotiate terms of surrender should the *coup d'etat* succeed. (He had no luck in securing such agreements.) Even while doing this work, Bonhoeffer started writing his *Ethics*. He envisioned it as his magnum opus, his most important work. Despite the fact that it was not finished when he died and that scholars disagree about the correct order of the completed sections, most regard it as such. The power of the text derives, in large part, from its rootedness in a real and burning question: What constitutes responsible Christian action in the world? In the context of Nazi Germany's "Final Solution" this was quite literally a question of life and death. Bonhoeffer did not write *Ethics* as an academic exercise in abstraction and speculation. For him the future of the church, Germany, Christianity, and humanity itself were at stake.

In this sense, Bonhoeffer's work is different than previous ethical formulations. He does not try to create rules or systems that might be good for all times and all places. Rather, he wants to address real problems facing real people, much like Luther did. Theologian John de Gruchy says most ethicists ask the question, "what does it mean to do good?" But that is the wrong (ethical) question for Bonhoeffer. The right one, strange as it might it might seem, is "what is the will of God?" In other words, de Gruchy explains, the real ethical question is this one: "what is it that, at this moment of our lives, we are required to do?" This question, asked while living under the threat of a blatantly evil government, makes sense. Bonhoeffer's answer, not surprisingly, resonates with the inherent tenets of Luther's theology of the cross.

Bonhoeffer claims that ethics is, what he calls, "conformation to Christ." It does not require that Christians try to emulate Jesus in their every action, but simply to live in the world as Jesus did, responding to the real needs of real humans.[28] Christ was really and concretely human,

---

28. "To be conformed to the one who has become human—that is what being human really means . . . to be conformed to the crucified—that means to be a human being judged by God . . . to be conformed to the risen one—that means to be a new human being before God . . . [to be conformed to Christ means] Jesus Christ taking form in Christ's church. The New Testament, in deep and clear indication of the matter itself, calls the church the body of Christ." Bonhoeffer, *Ethics*, DBWE 6:94–96.

committed to serving the needs of real humans in specific situations. In Bonhoeffer's case, the war, the vilification and annihilation of Jews and others, the co-opting of the church by proponents of Nazi ideology—all this required ethical action on the part of Christians. But the choices were difficult. Bonhoeffer's understanding of ethics as formation opened possibilities for responding to the needs of the people most terribly impacted. Bonhoeffer's resonance with Luther meant those responses could be offered freely, even if at great personal cost.

Without question, Bonhoeffer's call to ethical and responsible action is costly. Ethics as formation, grounded in his understanding of *Stellvertretung*, requires a willingness to suffer or, if necessary, take on guilt. (That is, do something that, even though it is the responsible thing to do in the given situation, is also a sinful act.) For Bonhoeffer, the only way to take responsible Christian action on behalf of the victims of the Nazi state was to participate in a plot to kill Hitler. He felt called, by God, to do it. But he never tried to justify murder or the killing of a tyrant "in this case." He maintained that he and his co-conspirators were, in fact, sinning. And so Bonhoeffer hoped and prayed for, he depended on, a God who demands such bold and sinful action but who "promises forgiveness and consolation" to the one who becomes a sinner in the process.[29] Here the interplay of grace and freedom, found first in Luther and then in Bonhoeffer, is key. Bonhoeffer's context demanded that he rethink traditional approaches to ethical decision making; his theology, particularly his Christology and radical understanding of grace, allowed him to do so. The Christian, conformed to Christ, acts and suffers on behalf of those in this world, especially those who are weak and suffering, powerless, and voiceless.

Can Christianity Be Religionless?

In April of 1943, Dietrich Bonhoeffer was arrested on tenuous charges related to a rescue mission—helping 14 Jews escape Germany—supported by the *Abwehr* and his ecumenical contacts in Switzerland. He was taken to Tegel Prison in Berlin. Confined to a 7 by 10 foot cell, Bonhoeffer made a commitment to make the best of his new circumstances. He created a daily routine of prayer, reading Scripture, exercise, and, perhaps most importantly, writing. Bonhoeffer's most profound and innovative theological

29. Bonhoeffer, "An Account," DBWE 8:41.

reflections, in particular, his reflections on "religionless Christianity," were penned in Tegel Prison.

Bonhoeffer wrote to his best friend, Eberhard Bethge, about theological matters weighing on his mind. "What keeps gnawing at me is the question, what is Christianity, or who is Christ actually for us today?" [30] He was convinced that the world had "come of age," that it was a religionless time, and he wondered what it meant, in such a time, to talk about justification, repentance, and faith. [31] But what began as a worry for Bonhoeffer resulted in a powerful theological discovery. His efforts to interpret Christianity for a "completely religionless time" produced an articulation of Christianity, or "religionless Christianity," which is nothing short of a radical reinterpretation of Christ as the coming of God into the world. Once again, the resonance of Bonhoeffer's thinking with the Luther's theology of the cross is striking.

The good news of religionless Christianity, for Bonhoeffer, is the good news of Jesus on the cross. Christ is with us and helps us, Bonhoeffer claims, not by power and omnipotence but by weakness and suffering. The one who is pushed out of the world and onto the cross is the one who is with us in our suffering. For Bonhoeffer, the difference between religion and Christianity parallels the difference between the long-standing, but false, concept of God as the stop-gap for the shortcomings of human knowledge and the desperate invocation of security and power, which trades upon human weakness, on the one hand, and the suffering Christ and the "following after" him by disciples, on the other hand. Bonhoeffer expresses the difference this way: "Human religiosity directs people in need to the power of God in the world . . . The Bible directs people toward the powerlessness and the suffering of God; only the suffering God can help."[32] To live in this world and share in the suffering of God is the call of each Christian. It is a call to live a "secular life." Luther understood this long before Bonhoeffer. No one is called or obliged to be religious in a particular way. But each one is called to follow after Christ, to participate in this life with all its political messiness. In his famous essay, "An Account at the Turn of the Year 1942–1943," Bonhoeffer emphatically notes that this world must not be dis-

---

30. Bonhoeffer, *Letters and Papers from Prison*, DBWE 8:362.

31. Ibid.: "The age when we could tell people that with words—whether theological or pious words—is past, as is the age of inwardness and of conscience, and that means the age of religion altogether. We are approaching a completely religionless age; people as they are now simply cannot be religious any more."

32. Ibid., 479.

missed out of hand. His point is to distinguish between those who count themselves religious and, in pious escapism, do nothing in the face of Nazi atrocities, and those who choose to embrace their responsibilities in the real and secular world, acting out their faith on behalf of future generations.

"Religious people speak of God," wrote Bonhoeffer, "at a point where human knowledge is at an end (or sometimes when they're too lazy to think further), or when human strength fails. Actually, it's a *deus ex machina* that they're always bringing on the scene, either to appear to solve insoluble problems or to provide strength when human powers fail, thus always exploiting human weakness or human limitations."[33] Bonhoeffer was distressed by the fact that God had come to be known primarily as one who answers unanswerable questions—one who waits in the wings, on the boundaries of life, to be ushered in during times of human failure. From Bonhoeffer's view, this image of God, this *deus ex machina*, was inappropriate, even dangerous.[34]

In discussing the possibility of a "religionless Christianity," then, Bonhoeffer wanted to rethink the place, image, and role of God in modern life. He writes, "I'd like to speak of God not at the boundaries but in the center, not in weakness but in strength, thus not in death and guilt but in human life and goodness."[35] Bonhoeffer's thinking reflects his reading of the New Testament and his appraisal of God's self-revelation in Jesus as the Christ who comes into the world to live among people, especially the weak and suffering. It also brings us back to Lutheran sensibilities embedded throughout his thinking and writing.

For Bonhoeffer, faith is something whole. It stands in contrast to religion or the religious act, which is something partial:

---

33. Ibid., 366.

34. *Deus ex machina*, or "god from the machine," is a term from ancient Greek and Roman theater. When characters faced irresolvable conflicts, a divine character dropped onto the stage by wires attached to pulleys (i.e., "the machine"), resolved the conflict, and exited swiftly and mysteriously. For many (so-called) religious people, Bonhoeffer contends, God functions in precisely this way. But God, in this view, must remain forever on the boundaries of human life and experience. Because humans find themselves increasingly able to answer questions on their own through scientific advancement or existential and psychological analysis, they are increasingly able to understand the world and themselves without recourse to God. Consequently, this God (or this image of God as *deus ex machina*) steadily becomes superfluous.

35. Bonhoeffer, *Letters and Papers from Prison*, DBWE 8:367.

Our lives must be "worldly," so that we can share precisely so in
God's suffering . . . Being Christian does not mean being religious
in a certain way . . . Instead it means being human, not a certain
type of human, but the human being that Christ creates in us. It is
not a religious act that makes someone Christian, but rather sharing in God's suffering in the worldly life . . . The "religious act" is
always something partial, whereas "faith" is something whole and
involves one's whole life. Jesus calls not to a new religion but to
life.[36]

Though this theme, which echoes the idea of the unity of reality, may be
familiar by now, it is no less radical. We find God at the center of our experience, not at the boundaries being pushed ever farther away. The words of
Bonhoeffer's letter to Bethge on July 21, 1944, resound with his realization
of "the profound this-worldliness of Christianity": "I discovered . . . that it
is only by living completely in this world that one learns to have faith." By
this-worldliness, he continues, "I mean living unreservedly in life's duties,
problems, successes, failures, experiences and perplexities."[37] In doing so,
says Bonhoeffer, we take seriously the sufferings of God in the world. We
can and we do watch with Christ in Gethsemane.

Does Obedience to God Require Death?[38]

On July 20, 1944, one day before Bonhoeffer wrote so eloquently to Bethge
about the this-worldliness of faith, the *Abwehr's* third and final attempt
to take Hitler's life failed. Col. Claus von Stauffenberg placed a bomb in a
briefcase under the table at the *Wolfsschanze*, or Wolf's Lair, for a briefing
between Hitler and high ranking Nazi officials. When the bomb exploded,
havoc ensued. The room was destroyed, four were dead, but Hitler emerged
unharmed. He declared himself invincible and his mission blessed by God.
A full-scale investigation ensued and documents naming all the members
of the conspiracy were discovered. Bonhoeffer's name was included. He
was moved from Tegel to several concentration camps until he arrived at

36. Ibid., 480, 482.

37. Ibid.

38. Recall the critical questions that Hughes poses to Kierkegaard about the role
of suffering and martyrdom within Christian faith in chapter 2 above. The following
chapter continues to examine the complex relationship between discipleship/vocation
and suffering/death.

Flossenbürg in the spring of 1945. The Third Reich was about to fall, and Hitler wanted to make sure members of the conspiracy did not survive. He personally ordered the execution of Bonhoeffer. On April 7, a summary court-martial was held and Bonhoeffer was sentenced to death. Early in the morning on April 9, 1945, Bonhoeffer was hanged.

Some years later, the camp doctor who witnessed Bonhoeffer's death wrote:

> On the morning of that day between five and six o'clock the prisoners . . . were taken from their cells and the verdicts of the court martial read out to them. Through the half-open door in one room of the huts I saw Pastor Bonhoeffer, before taking off his prison garb, kneeling on the floor praying fervently to his God. I was most deeply moved by the way this unusually lovable man prayed, so devout and so certain that God heard his prayer. At the place of execution, he again said a short prayer and then climbed the steps to the gallows, brave and composed. His death ensued after a few seconds. In the almost fifty years that I worked as a doctor, I have hardly ever seen a man die so entirely submissive to the will of God.[39]

In a broken world come of age, Dietrich Bonhoeffer's sensibilities and theology not only allowed, but required, him to follow after Christ in a radical political vocation that cost him his life. A Lutheran radical, and radically Lutheran, Bonhoeffer continues to challenge us to pay attention to the world around us, to act freely on behalf of others, and to act boldly, and even radically, when called to do so.

---

39. Bethge, *Dietrich Bonhoeffer*, 851.

For Further Reading (and Viewing)

Bethge, Renate. *Dietrich Bonhoeffer: A Brief Life*. Translated by K. C. Hanson. Minneapolis: Fortress, 2004.

Bonhoeffer: Pastor, Pacifist, Nazi Resister. Directed by Martin Doblmeier. 2003. Journey Films Production. 2004. DVD.

Come before Winter. Directed by Kevin Ekvall. 2017. DVD.

Green, Clifford, and Michael DeJonge. *The Bonhoeffer Reader*. Minneapolis: Fortress, 2013.

Haynes, Stephen, and Lori Brandt Hale. *Bonhoeffer for Armchair Theologians*. Louisville: Westminster John Knox, 2009.

Schlingenseipen, Ferdinand. *Dietrich Bonhoeffer 1906–1945: Martyr, Thinker, Man of Resistance*. Translated by Isabel Best. New York: T. & T. Clark, 2010.

Discussion Questions

1. In what ways does contemporary North American culture continue to separate "private" religion from public/political responsibilities, as Lutheran understandings of the two kingdoms were understood to do in the early twentieth century? Do such separations continue to support the status quo? How might Bonhoeffer's reconsiderations help point the way forward?

2. Bonhoeffer, like Kierkegaard, critiques Lutherans and other Christians for confusing "free grace" with "cheap grace." How is grace taken for granted or confused with privilege and latitude by Christians whom you know? How might the importance of discipleship be restored?

3. Are Christians ever called to civil disobedience? When and how might they hear and heed such a calling?

4. What do you make of Bonhoeffer's provocative claim that, in a world come of age, "only a suffering God can help?"

4

Dorothee Soelle

Lutheran Liberation Theologian of the Cross

Jacqueline Bussie

"My life is that of a theological worker who tries to tell
something of God's pain and God's joy." —Dorothee Soelle[1]

Those who grasp the rich depths of the life and work of Dorothee Soelle
(1929–2003) refer to her by many names—mystic, mother, activist, rebel,
theologian, professor, poet, prophet, feminist, socialist. However, the label
"Lutheran" is not among the common designations used to describe Soelle.
In *Dorothee Soelle—Mystic and Rebel*, Renate Wind, Soelle's biographer,
never mentions the term in reference to Soelle.[2] This strange omission
throughout the literature on Soelle gives the unfair impression that she
had no relationship to the Lutheran theology that was interwoven within
her own cultural and religious heritage, a perspective that this chapter will
argue is false and misleading.

Scholars perhaps eschew the appellation "Lutheran" because Soelle, as
a liberation theologian, incessantly critiqued the Protestant church of her
heritage—the Evangelical (Lutheran) Church in Germany—and because
this conservative Lutheran church often condemned Soelle's views. Rather
than take this facile approach, I argue instead for a clear-eyed recognition

1. Soelle, *Against the Wind*, 166.
2. Wind, *Dorothee Soelle*.

that a contentious relationship is nonetheless still just that—a relationship. As a church bishop friend of Soelle's affirmed during Soelle's memorial service, "Dorothee was a church woman, despite all assertions to the contrary."[3]

Dorothee Soelle was born in 1929 in Cologne, Germany, and died in 2003 from a heart attack. She was married twice, and had four children. World War II, Nazism, Hitler, and the Holocaust shaped her childhood and adolescence, and led Soelle to wrestle throughout her entire life with shame over and disenchantment with her own culture. Fascinated with questions of faith, political movements, and ethical responsibility, Soelle earned her Ph.D. from the University of Cologne in theology, philosophy, and literature. She published her first theological text, *Christ the Representative*, in 1965, and proceeded to publish over twenty-four theological books and dozens of articles during the next forty years. Scholars frequently compare Soelle's unsystematic theological writings to Martin Luther's, noting that she primarily addressed real-life events and concerns that arose rather than striving to be systematic.[4] Because of her outspoken criticism of her country and its government, history, and national church, Soelle never received a professor position at a German university. She was, however, a beloved professor at Union Theological Seminary in New York for over a decade (1975–87).

During the course of her career as a theologian, teacher, and political activist, Soelle became well-known for her pacifism and socialism, as well as for her active participation in the peace movement, Christian-Marxist dialogue, anti-war and anti-nuclear protests, and the Latin American liberation theology movement. Though many would disagree with her activism, it is important to grasp that Soelle personally understood her participation in all of these movements as a form of lived theology, as a way of living out the gospel and following Jesus—a social revolutionary—in the twentieth century. For Soelle, all of these controversial movements foregrounded care for the least and most vulnerable among us—a task with which Jesus charged all of his followers, and which Soelle took seriously. Though Soelle critiqued the church and its acceptance of the status quo, she was forever captivated by and compelled by the love of Jesus. Writes Soelle, "I did not intend to 'come home' to church, since I mistrusted the institution deeply. I went home to Pascal and Kierkegaard, to the early Luther—all of them

---

3. Pinnock, *The Theology of Dorothee Soelle*, ix.
4. Soelle, *Essential Writings*, 28.

being homeless in the established churches."[5] Soelle's rejection of much of the church establishment, therefore, should not be mistaken for a rejection of the Christian gospel or of Jesus—or even of the church per se. As this chapter will show through an exploration of Soelle's theology, Soelle, like Luther, sought to reform her tradition, not to reject it.

Luther's theology and the work of later Lutherans, especially Dietrich Bonhoeffer, profoundly influenced Soelle's own theology. In the tradition of Martin Luther and the Reformation's dictum *"ecclesia semper reformanda est"* (the church is always reforming), Soelle is best understood as a twentieth-century reformer engaged in the perennial gift and task of the Reformation tradition. Like the many reformers before her, Soelle labored tirelessly to re-form the church for continued relevance and a renewed ability to address the world's urgent needs of the day. Soelle understood her own work in precisely this way, as she wrote in her theological memoir: "I often experienced liberation theology as a reformation in Europe . . . A new theological thinking accompanies this *ecclesia semper reformanda*."[6]

As a corrective to the gap in studying and understanding Soelle's relationship to Lutheran theology, this chapter will look at Soelle with fresh twenty-first-century eyes and ask: How is Dorothee Soelle's theology distinctly Lutheran? Where do Soelle's and Luther's key ideas intersect, and where do they diverge? How does Soelle fit Luther's definition of a theologian of the cross? How does Soelle radicalize, transform, revolutionize, and reinterpret the Lutheran tradition for a modern context? In other words, how is Soelle a radical Lutheran and/or a Lutheran radical?

I will argue that according to Luther's seminal definition of the term *theologia crucis* (theology of the cross) in the Heidelberg Disputation, Dorothee Soelle is a theologian of the cross par excellence. I will argue in particular that Soelle inherits and adopts Luther's understanding and use of the theological concepts of *deus absconditus in passionibus* (God's hiddenness in suffering), sin defined as *homo incurvatus in se ipsum* (the human being turned in upon him/herself), and "calling things by their right names" (prophetic critique). The chapter will reveal the ways in which Soelle reworks and radicalizes these distinctive aspects of traditional Lutheran thought regarding the *theologica crucis*, not only making them her own but also revivifying them for relevance and liberative praxis in the twenty-first century. Based on this evidence, I will conclude that we best

5. Ibid., 21.

6. Soelle, *Against the Wind*, 102.

reimagine Soelle as a Lutheran liberation theologian of the cross—a title that both names Soelle's real indebtedness to her Lutheran predecessors such as Luther and Bonhoeffer and acknowledges the rigorous extent to which she radicalized their thought through creative adaptation for liberation theology.

God Hidden and Revealed in Suffering

In the Heidelberg Disputation (1518), Luther first coined the term theologian of the cross, which he set over and against a theologian of glory. In that text, he pioneered the following definition of a theologian of the cross:

> That person does not deserve to be called a theologian who looks upon the invisible things of God as though they were clearly perceptible in those things which have actually happened (Rom 1:20).
>
> He deserves to be called a theologian, however, who comprehends the visible and manifest things of God seen through suffering and the cross.[7]

In his explanation to Thesis 20, Luther explains that the

> visible things of God are placed in opposition to the invisible, namely, his human nature, weakness, foolishness . . . Because men misused the knowledge of God through works, God wished again to be recognized in suffering, and to condemn wisdom concerning invisible things by means of wisdom concerning visible things, so that those who did not honor God as manifested in his works should honor him as he is hidden in his suffering [absconditum in passionibus] . . . Now it is not sufficient for anyone, and it does [the theologian] no good to recognize God in his glory and majesty, unless he recognizes him in the humility and shame of the cross.[8]

A theologian of the cross comprehends the paradox of God's hiddenness and, in particular, of God's hiddenness in suffering and on the cross. Luther continues with his following thesis:

> A theology of glory calls evil good and good evil. A theology of the cross calls the thing what it actually is.[9]

7. Luther, "Heidelberg Disputation," *BTW* 57 (theses 19 and 20).
8. Ibid., 57 (explanation of thesis 20).
9. Ibid., 58 (thesis 21).

He then explains:

> This is clear: He who does not know Christ does not know God hidden in suffering. Therefore he prefers works to suffering, glory to the cross, strength to weakness, wisdom to folly, and, in general, good to evil. These are the people whom the apostle calls "enemies of the cross of Christ" (Phil. 3:18), for they hate the cross and suffering and love works and the glory of works. Thus they call the good of the cross evil and the evil of a deed good. God can be found only in suffering and the cross, as has already been said."[10]

Whereas a theologian of glory appears to get just about everything backward, the theologian of the cross publicly calls a "thing what it actually is." She or he uses prophetic critique to distinguish between good and evil and help others discern God's will.

Sounds clear enough. But for Luther, the idea that one can find God "hidden" in suffering and the cross leads to all sorts of paradoxical, if also powerful, "insights." In fact, the Heidelberg Disputation registered several seminal ideas that eventually functioned as telltale watermarks on the pages of the Lutheran tradition. The first of these is the notion of *deus absconditus*, the hidden God. In describing God as hidden in this treatise, Luther cited the unsettling, often-ignored verse found in the Hebrew Bible: "Truly you are a God who hides himself, O God of Israel" (Isaiah 45:15).[11]

While the notion of God in hiding may strike some as strange and heretical, I would argue that in describing God this way, Luther drew not only upon the Scriptures but also upon his own lifelong authentic struggles with "theodicy," or "the problem of evil." Though variable in severity from person to person, encounters with evil and suffering are arguably universal. For Luther, these and all of our experiences should play a valid role when we "do theology." And who among us when we have suffered an incomprehensible sorrow or evil has not asked ourselves: "Where is God?" Even Jesus himself on the cross felt abandoned by God and therefore cried out, "My God, my God, why have you forsaken me?" (Matt 27:46).[12]

The world over, encounters with radical suffering make human beings feel in their very bones the incomprehensible hiddenness—even the perceived absence—of God. At such moments, God seems evanescent, inaccessible, and unreachable, like clouds in the sky appear to those whose

---

10. Ibid. (explanation of thesis 21).

11. Ibid., 57 (explanation of thesis 20).

12. See chapter 1 for an account of Luther's pivotal interpretation of this verse.

feet stand on all-too-solid ground. Holocaust survivor Simon Wiesenthal remarks that, in the midst of life's cruelties, many feel that God is "on leave."[13] Another Holocaust survivor and Nobel peace prize winner, Elie Wiesel, recounts in his memoir *Night* a wretched day in Auschwitz when he was forced to watch the hanging of an 8 year-old child. The grisly execution prompts Wiesel to ask, "Where is God now?" and to answer, "Here He is—He is hanging here on this gallows."[14]

One might draw a fairly straight line from Luther's pronouncement of God as fully revealed on the cross to Wiesel's anguished question concerning whether God is not absent or even dead in light of the Shoah[15]—God as hanging on the gallows.[16] We tend to forget that the cross was not first of all a shiny symbol of Christian victory, ready-made for jewelry or pious art, but rather a menacing sign of the Roman Empire's power to torture and execute political insurrectionists. We should also note that Jesus's crucifixion has for centuries gruesomely served as Christian justification for anti-Semitism, as many Christians have mistakenly (and grotesquely) argued that Jews must be rejected and punished because they are responsible for Jesus's death.

Soelle herself is part of the chain of thought that moves from Golgotha through Auschwitz. As a German child who grew up during the final years of the Nazi regime, Soelle was intensely ashamed by Auschwitz and forever haunted by its inescapable ethical and theological questions. Asked Soelle, "How could this happen? What did my parents do to stop it?" Knowing of Luther's anti-Jewish writings, she asked: "Did Martin Luther play a part?" She "tried to develop a 'post-Auschwitz' theology"; she did not want "to write one sentence in which the awareness of that greatest catastrophe of [her] people was not made explicit."[17] Both the notion of God as the hidden God and God as hidden in suffering lie at the epicenter of Soelle's groundbreaking post-Auschwitz theology; she inherited both from Luther. Soelle

13. Wiesenthal, *The Sunflower*, 8.

14. Wiesel, *Night*, 62.

15. Many contemporary Jews prefer the term "Shoah" (literally, the "catastrophe") over "holocaust" (a biblical term referring to a "burnt offering") to refer to the genocide in northern Europe in the 1940s.

16. Those who have drawn this line from Luther to Wiesel, including Moltmann, *The Crucified God*, 273–78, can and have been criticized for "Christianizing the holocaust," projecting onto it a meaning or even meaningfulness that it does not have. See the discussion in Carroll, *Constantine's Sword*, 3–12.

17. Soelle, *Against the Wind*, 16.

states: "God . . . is not the all-powerful conqueror but stands instead on the side of the poor and disadvantaged—*a God who is always hidden in the world* and wants to become visible."[18] The comparison here with Luther and the Heidelberg Disputation is obvious.

Indeed, Soelle's entire work as a theologian draws heavily upon Luther's revolutionary claim that the God whom Christians worship is a God who suffers, a God who allows Godself to be humiliated and even shamed on the cross. Luther's God is clearly not the God of Western philosophy.[19] To use Luther's own Latin phrase, God hides *sub contrario*, under an opposite sign. God hides within pain, vulnerability, suffering, and "weakness." Writes Soelle, "God could not comfort us if She were not bound to us in pain . . . All suffering persons are in the presence of God."[20]

Soelle differs from Luther, however, in that she ultimately took Luther's initial concepts of *sub contrario* and God's hiddenness in suffering to their radical limits through two unique additional assertions—namely, that God hides and therefore resides among the poor and dispossessed and that the cross reveals that God is powerless and therefore in need of human help.

God's Hiddenness among the Poor and Marginalized

The first way Soelle pushes the envelope on Luther's understanding of *deus absconditus* is to argue that God is not only found hidden on the cross, but also among the poor and disenfranchised. If God hides under God's opposite, Soelle reasons, then God must "hide" in those whom the world considers weak, foolish, outcast, and unrespectable. If God is hidden in suffering, then God hides within those who suffer, and in particular those within our global society who collectively suffer the most—people who live in poverty and marginalization. In order best to honor God in God's suffering, we must then honor, serve, and suffer with the poor. For in the poor, we find Christ, as Christ himself said in Matt 25:45: "Truly I tell you, just as you did not do it to one of the least of these, you did not do it to me." In the eyes of the world, the poor are useless, abandoned by God. Yet for Soelle, who faithfully practices Luther's admonition to see God *sub contrario* in

18. Soelle, *Theology for Skeptics*, 17. Italics mine.

19. This is another way to make sense of Bonhoeffer's distinction between religion and "religionless" Christianity; see chapter 3 above.

20. Soelle, *Theology for Skeptics*, 72.

suffering, the poor are Jesus's homestead. Jesus is the poor's *alma mater*, in the literal sense of the term. He is their bounteous mother, the One who feeds their hunger. Soelle considers God's hiddenness amongst the poor and the suffering to be one of the greatest paradoxes of the Christian faith: "God must also be thought of as present with those who are in misery . . . The paradox [is] that God loves us even when nothing of that is visible."[21]

For Luther, Golgotha alone made manifest an empathic God,[22] but for Soelle any and all human suffering—especially that of the poor and oppressed—can mediate God's presence. While Luther expressed a marvelous confidence that God was found in the most unlikely place—the humiliation of the cross—he largely failed to take the next step of identifying God's presence in the equally unlikely contemporary socio-economic crucifixions of the disenfranchised who live in the humiliation and shame of poverty.

In making this statement, I by no means want to imply that Luther gave no thought to the destitute. As Samuel Torvend has convincingly argued, Luther did indeed care about the poor.[23] A primary reason Luther protested the sale of indulgences was his belief that through such sales, the wealthy papacy exploited the poor. Additionally, Luther wrote moving passages regarding our Christian duty to care for those in need: "As love and support are given you, you in turn must render love and support to Christ in his needy ones. You must feel with sorrow all the dishonor done to Christ in his holy Word, all the misery of Christendom, all the unjust suffering of the innocent, with which the world is everywhere overflowing."[24] While compassionate toward the poor, Luther neglected to fully forge the theological connection between God's hiding *sub contrario* and God's hiddenness within the poor. Liberation theologians such as Soelle take up that task centuries later, but they grow this tree from roots that Luther himself helped plant.

Liberation theology originated among the poor in Latin America in the 1950s and 1960s, and was adopted (and adapted) by various oppressed groups around the world. The father of liberation theology, Peruvian

21. Soelle, *Suffering*, 165.

22. However, there is some compelling, inviting slippage in Luther's language. In thesis 20 of the Heidelberg Disputation, Luther writes of God revealed in the cross of Jesus and in (his) suffering—sometimes specifying that the suffering is "his" (that is, Jesus's) and sometimes leaving suffering undefined. Luther, "Heidelberg Disputation," *BTW* 57; compare *LW* 31:52–53.

23. Besides chapter 1 above, see Torvend, *Luther and the Hungry Poor*.

24. Luther, "The Sacrament of the Body," *BTW* 247.

Catholic priest Gustavo Gutierrez, first coined the term in 1971, in the context of speaking out against the terrible injustices, abuses of power, and rampant poverty in the region. Liberation theology discerns in the gospel a call to concrete action, a call to liberate the poor, marginalized, and vulnerable from the social, political, and economic conditions that shackle these beloved children of God. Liberation theology does not foreground an afterlife in which injustice will be rectified, but instead urges all the faithful, as followers of Jesus, to actively seek justice in the here-and-now.[25] Liberation theology takes as its primary mantra the wisdom of Jeremiah 22:13: "to know God is to do justice." In its vision, not only do the oppressed work for their own liberation, but also the privileged struggle alongside them in solidarity.[26]

Liberation theology is heavily influenced by Karl Marx, who argued that the material conditions of people's lives must be addressed and that society's current capitalist structure intentionally disenfranchises the poor and creates intolerable inequities between the haves and have-nots. Firmly grounded in the book of Exodus and its story of the liberation of the Jewish people from Pharoah's enslavement, liberation theology argues that God has a "preferential option for the poor," meaning that God is actively at work in the world on the side of the poor and the oppressed, empowering them to attain their freedom and liberation. Gutierrez and other liberation theologians are clear in their insistence that God's love is universal. They argue, however, that because the actual, sinful world daily enacts a preferential option for the rich, a preferential option for the poor is needed in order to restore balance and authentic equity.[27]

Unlike Luther, and unlike Kierkegaard, for whom Christ and Christ's cross are always scandalously unique and particular, for Soelle, the cross is not a one-time event but a perennial process in which God resides. In her autobiographical words, "I began to understand God becoming human no longer as a unique, completed event, but as an ongoing process in history.

25. Compare Bonhoeffer's focus on "this worldly" Christianity as explored in chapter 3 above.

26. Brown, *Liberation Theology*, 66. This text is an excellent introduction to liberation theology for those who would like to learn more.

27. Liberation theology's "preferential option for the poor" is controversial, and its original detractors insistently counter-argued that "God loves everyone equally" (something liberation theology has not denied). At the time of this writing, I am struck by the ideological similarity between liberation theology's detractors and the contemporary detractors of the Black Lives Matter movement who argue "all lives matter."

In this process God is rendered invisible (as in Auschwitz), or is made manifest in the experience of liberation."[28] For Soelle, Christ is crucified not just on Golgatha, but every day that we marginalize or disenfranchise other human beings across the globe. Soelle explains: "The cross is no theological invention, but the world's answer, given a thousand times over, to attempts at liberation . . . De facto love ends up on the cross and within visible reality God chooses to act paradoxically."[29]

Soelle believes that "crucifixions" of the oppressed and the poor in our global society indicate God's presence because, paradoxically, crucifying assaults on the marginalized's dignity occur precisely where liberation and the kingdom of God attempt to break into our world. In Soelle's vision, suffering is a labor pain of the kingdom of God as it struggles to be born within our systems of greed, hate, and domination, which of course exerts every effort to quash its birth. Those who seek to birth justice in an unjust world will inevitably suffer and share in God's pain. Soelle writes: "Liberation theology taught me to understand the Bible not only as a summons to do God's will in a world of injustice, but also as a summons to endure discrimination, difficulties, and—certainly in many places in developing countries—martyrdom."[30]

Soelle radically reinterprets redemption not as mere eschatological hope—something that only happens in the end time—but as something that happens everywhere, all the time, especially when we feel at our most disappointed and defeated, during "the dark night of the world."[31] Writes Soelle, "The crying and groaning Paul speaks of [in Galatians 4:19] refers to the last days of giving birth; it is a labor of hope of those who in the hopelessness of this world wait for God. The Messiah does not come without the labor pains of messianic time . . . We need a different theology of pain that . . . relate[s] our pain to the pain of God . . . This pain is a sacrament, a sign of God's presence."[32] In Soelle's theology, the crucifixion of Jesus happens every day, but so does the resurrection. The "resurrection" happens each and every time the marginalized assert their dignity and when those who

28. Soelle, *Against the Wind*, 50.

29. Soelle, *Suffering*, 164.

30. Soelle, *Against the Wind*, 99. Compare Kierkegaard's portrayal of martyrdom and the critical comments by Hughes in chapter 2 above.

31. Soelle uses this phrase in *The Silent Cry*, 147.

32. Ibid., 78.

are not disenfranchised accompany them in their work toward liberation: "Where there is solidarity there is resurrection."[33]

Soelle's radical claims of resurrection birth pangs remind me of the June 17, 2015 racial terrorism attack on the Emanuel AME Church in Charleston, South Carolina. On that day, a white teenager walked into a Bible study and, after expressing hatred of African Americans, murdered nine black people with a handgun. In the days that followed, I was amazed to see this mind-numbing, horrible event result swiftly in the redemptive removal of the Confederate flag from not only South Carolina's statehouse but also other statehouses across the south—a removal for which countless brave African Americans and their civil rights allies of all races had sought passionately for over fifty years.

Though it would be naïve and dangerous to claim that these innocent deaths were necessary or therefore justified by this outcome, in this case Soelle's paradoxical thesis that redemption can break in at the moment of terror seems undeniably apropos. The murdered nine shared in God's pain; their visible suffering made manifest God's invisible presence within and alongside all those who suffer our nation's racial injustice. Soelle (who loved frequently to quote the mystic St. John of the Cross and is considered a mystic herself) writes that "that eternal spring lies hidden/How well I know its hiding place/Even when it is night."[34]

Toward a Liberating Lutheran Political Theology

As our discussion thus far makes clear, Soelle differs from Luther significantly in that for her, *every* theological idea possesses clear socio-political implications and consequences: "Every theological statement has to be at the same time a political one."[35] For Luther there are two kingdoms—one divine, and one human—although both are ruled by God and can never be completely separated, as Luther and especially Bonhoeffer make clear. Yet, for Soelle there is decidedly only one realm: the kingdom of God on earth that God wants our help to usher in.

For Soelle, then, *deus absconditum in passionibus* (God hidden in suffering) carries clear socio-political weight. In Soelle's theology, if God is hidden in the poor and the oppressed, then liberation theology is the

33. Soelle, *Essential Writings*, 136.

34. Soelle, *The Silent Cry*, 143.

35. Soelle, *Against the Wind*, 38.

only fitting option for faithful Christians truly seeking to follow Christ in today's world. Liberation theology argues, of course, that to know God is to do justice and this because God has a preferential option for the poor. Solidarity with the poor and the oppressed must function as the touchstone of the Christian life. In a bitter twist of irony, however, by extending Luther's hidden-God concept to its logical conclusion, Soelle ends up making a clean break with the dominant implementation of Luther's politics and social ethics, which cannot, in most cases, be described as liberationist.

To cite the most glaring historical example, consider the fact that Luther unequivocally condemned the German Peasant War (1524–25), in which thousands of impoverished and overtaxed peasants rose up and fought for their political and legal rights. Many of these peasants were inspired by Luther's own revolutionary theology to seek justice and equality, but Luther described the peasants' revolt as the work of the devil.[36] In stark contrast, Soelle argued that Jesus *was* the peasant in the German Peasant's War.[37] Inexplicably to many Lutherans, Luther failed in this crucial situation and in many others (most embarrassingly in his despicable anti-Judaism) to move from his own theological theory to ethical and political praxis. It saddens me that a theologian who argued for the priesthood of all believers—a radically egalitarian and democratic notion—could reject the peasant's struggle for equality with such utter contempt. Even Soelle credits Luther's idea of the priesthood of all believers as a cornerstone upon which the poor felt empowered enough to develop liberation theology![38]

As a Lutheran theologian, I choose to be completely honest about Luther's mistakes rather than to pretend otherwise. In doing so, I take my inspiration from Luther, who was always unafraid to critique authority and other people's theological ideas. I always tell my students that we can and should critique Luther and, ironically, we know that we can and should because none other than Luther taught us how.

As twenty-first-century Christians, we cannot make use of many of Luther's theological ideas. We must not only reject ideas like Luther's anti-Judaism, but also repent of them. Other ideas of Luther's can enrich our lives and nurture our faith in marvelously impactful ways. Such is the

36. See Lohse, *Martin Luther's Theology*, 159.

37. See Soelle, *Theology for Skeptics*, 95.

38. See Soelle, *Against the Wind*, 103. "The truly new impulses of Christianity come from very different places, for example, from the slums somewhere in Brazil . . . The base-communities have created new cultural forms . . . They discovered the priesthood of all believers."

paradox of Luther and his ambiguous bequest to us; fortunately, Lutheran thought embraces paradox. In the case of the influential theological concept of *deus absconditum in passionibus*, Luther birthed it; Soelle mothered it into a productive, active life of justice-seeking and liberative praxis our consciences can embrace with admiration rather than shame. While Luther urged us to become theologians of the cross, Soelle challenged us to go one step beyond that and become liberation theologians of the cross—not only to see God with those who suffer, but also to join in solidarity with them for the freeing and empowerment of the poor and oppressed.

Social and Economic Structures Turned in upon Themselves

Luther most likely failed to complete his half turn toward socio-political praxis because he held a more Augustinian understanding of sin as an individual's failure to do God's will. Indeed, Luther famously defined sin as *homo incurvatus in se ipsum*, or "the human person twisted/curved in upon her-/himself."[39] Soelle clearly valued Luther's definition, for she cites it repeatedly within her own work.[40] However, she insisted we move beyond its narrow individualism in our application. Soelle argued that just like individuals, communities can also be curved in upon themselves, resulting in phenomena such as nationalism, which sets one country against another in perpetual oppositional self-interest, and capitalism, which pits the rich against the poor. Writes Soelle in her memoir, "Of course I am aware of individual sins of which I accuse myself but . . . What I suffer from and what I need and seek forgiveness for, are all the disastrous things that we, as a society, inflict today on the poorest of the poor and on our mother, the earth."[41] For many Christians, this notion of collective sin is a troubling and new idea. Corporate and systemic sins such as racism, sexism, and nationalism are largely invisible to those who do not suffer their painful consequences. Our complicity hides even from ourselves, making it easy to eschew personal accountability.

39. See Bayer, *Martin Luther's Theology*, 183.

40. See these three examples: Soelle, *Mystery of Death*, 6; *Memoir of a Radical Christian*, 162; and *The Silent Cry*, 213.

41. Soelle, *Against the Wind*, 31. Whether humanity's typical anthropocentrism—its regard for human over non-human species—constitutes an additional "turning in" will be discussed in chapter 5 below.

In spite of these difficulties, Soelle adopts a more sociological perspective that underscores sin as a collective and systemic failure to do God's will. Luther understands sin predominantly from a personal perspective, whereas Soelle understands sin primarily from a structural perspective. Argues Soelle, "God's message is unambiguous: 'You are to feed the hungry, clothe the naked, bury the dead, visit the imprisoned.' All of these works are forbidden by the economic structure in which we live. It is designed to let the hungry starve, make the rich richer and the poor poorer."[42] She further adds: "God is justice. To know God means to do justice . . . Not until one understands murder by omission, or theft in terms of unjust prices for primary resources, does one recognize that we do steal from the poor and kill them."[43]

Of course, Lutherans (with many other Christians) regularly confess their complicity in structural evil. They speak of the things they have "left undone" (sins of omission) in addition to the things they have done (sins of commission). What is more, they repeat—for example, in the liturgy of Holy Baptism—their collective bondage to the transpersonal powers of Sin (with a capital S), death, and the devil. The question is whether many or any of them connect what sound like mythological entities to the very real—the very material—conditions that entrap and ensnare so many. One also wonders whether confession and repentance provide an adequate response to anything other than more "personal" sins. For Soelle, compassionate activism that works toward systemic change is the liberationist answer to structural sin: "[A politics of love] signifies a politicization of conscience, in utter contrast to our customary Christian education: it is so very busy privatizing our spiritual strength, to anchor it in the family and the individual. This arrests spiritual strength on the level of charity as interpreted by the bourgeois within us. Love that . . . does not dare to search mercilessly for the foundation of terror is not love."[44]

Soelle's re-understanding of sin as systemic is radical in the real sense of the term. While in common parlance we use the word radical to mean very new and different, or having extreme or fanatical views not shared by most people, the word radical literally means "a return to the roots," as the introduction to this book already made clear. While many of Soelle's ideas

---

42. Ibid., 99. Compare Luther's critique of the mercantile capitalism that was emerging in the sixteenth century, as discussed in chapter 1 above.

43. Ibid., 103.

44. Ibid., 136.

were wildly unpopular among her more traditional Christian counterparts, I would argue they were not radical in the sense of being new. Soelle's understanding of sin is radical in that her understanding returns to its Jewish roots. For although the Protestant tradition, following in Luther's footsteps, takes a largely personal perspective on sin, the prophets in the Hebrew Bible understood sin (and righteousness) in both collective and individual terms. This historical fact enables Soelle to argue with confidence: "We do believe, however, that the task of social criticism has thus far not been sufficiently recognized by the churches and by Christians. In practicing such a critique of our society we pursue an aspect of the Bible and the faith that's been neglected until now."[45]

God's "Powerlessness" and Need for Humanity

Soelle pushed the notion of *deus absconditus* to its limit in a second way when she further developed the radical notion of divine powerlessness as proposed by Lutheran pastor and Nazi resister Dietrich Bonhoeffer (1906–1945). Indeed, Soelle repeatedly engaged Dietrich Bonhoeffer in her work. Bonhoeffer, like Soelle, drank from the wells of Luther's thought but transformed it in order to better slake the thirst of the modern era. Soelle's biographer goes so far as to claim that Soelle had a "lifelong dialogue with Dietrich Bonhoeffer."[46] She embraced Bonhoeffer's definition of Jesus as "the human being for others," the one who stands in solidarity with the suffering, poor, and oppressed. Bonhoeffer's significant influence upon Soelle is further evidence of Soelle's active engagement with the Lutheran tradition.

In order to analyze how Soelle reworked Bonhoeffer, we must first discuss how Bonhoeffer himself first radicalized Luther. Though Luther insisted upon God's hiddenness *sub contrario*, he nonetheless clung to the notion of God's omnipotence. In other words, though God hid within weakness and humiliation, God was not *actually* weak. For Luther nothing happened in the world that the almighty God did not ordain: "Because God moves and accomplishes everything, he by necessity moves and accomplishes things also in Satan and in the godless . . . God cannot lay aside his omnipotence."[47]

45. Wind, *Mystic and Rebel*, 63.
46. Ibid., 44.
47. Luther, "The Bondage of the Will," as quoted in Bayer, 201.

In stark contrast to these claims of divine omnipotence, Bonhoeffer argued that God voluntarily became powerless upon the cross. Clearly summoning Luther's paradoxical *theologia crucis* but already radicalizing it, Bonhoeffer wrote the following provocative statement from behind the bars of his Nazi prison cell, which Lori Hale has already quoted, but which warrants quoting again:

> God would have us know that we must live as those who manage their lives without God . . . Before God, and with God, we live without God. God consents to be pushed out of the world and onto the cross; God is weak and powerless in the world and in precisely this way, and only so, is at our side and helps us . . . The Bible directs people toward the powerlessness and suffering of God; only the suffering God can help.[48]

Bonhoeffer also asserts that Christians today must discern Christ's presence in the weak and powerless, and therefore must learn "to see the great events of world history from below, from the perspective of the outcasts, the suspects, the maltreated, the powerless, the oppressed and reviled, in short from the perspective of the suffering."[49] Bonhoeffer concludes that given God's voluntary impotence in world affairs, we can be Christians today in only two ways—through prayer and by doing justice among human beings.[50]

We can see to what depths Soelle took Bonhoeffer's advice to heart. In Soelle's reflections on Bonhoeffer, she wrote: "If there is a theological-political continuity, it exists for me in this setting out anew with that powerless and suffering One present among us . . . To be with him . . . and follow him, means to make his perspective on life one's own."[51] Unfortunately, the Nazis cut Dietrich Bonhoeffer's life short, leaving little time for him to develop further his notion of God's powerlessness—a task that Soelle arguably took upon herself.

Soelle radicalized Bonhoeffer's notion of divine powerlessness with her explicit contention that if God is powerless, then God needs us as much as we need God. For most Christians, this line of thought runs contrary to all that they have learned about the divine-human relationship. In traditional Christian doctrine and teachings, God is omnipotent and needs

48. Bonhoeffer, *Letters and Papers from Prison*, DBWE 8:478–79.

49. Bonhoeffer, "An Account," in *Letters and Papers from Prison*, DBWE 8:52.

50. Bonhoeffer, *Letters and Papers from Prison*, DBWE 8:389.

51. Quoted in Wind, *Mystic and Rebel*, 45–46.

nothing at all from human beings—think of that verse in the song, "Jesus Loves Me," which says, "for they are weak and He [God] is strong." But in Soelle's theology, God needs our help to bring about redemption, liberation, and healing. God has empowered us to become co-creators with God. In this train of thought we witness Soelle's return to the roots of Jesus's own tradition of Judaism, which teaches that God calls humans to the task of *tikkun-olam*, to mend the world. Once again, Soelle's radicalism is radical in the literal sense of the term.

When I give presentations on Dorothee Soelle's theology at Lutheran churches, in order to teach Soelle's concept of divine powerlessness I often share these lines from her controversial poem "When He Came":

> He needs you
> that's all there is to it
> without you he's left hanging
> goes up in Dachau's smoke
> . . .
> gets revalued in the next stock market crash
> he's consumed and blown away
> used up
> without you
> Help him
> that's what faith is
> he can't bring it about
> his kingdom
> couldn't then couldn't later can't now
> not at any rate without you.[52]

Without fail, many in the congregation take deep offense to this poem. Tellingly, they do so by expressing that Soelle's God-needs-us claim contradicts Luther's foundational teaching that we are saved by faith and never by works. God does not need anything from us, they argue, especially not for our own salvation or liberation. Perhaps Luther likewise would find Soelle's post-Auschwitz radical translation of *deus absconditus in passionis* into divine powerlessness and neediness to smack of a works-righteousness.

But Soelle, unlike Luther, rejected the traditional view of God as omnipotent. She contended that this belief disempowered human beings and fostered quietism through a fatalistic acceptance of the status quo as God's will. (Luther's own poor example supports this argument—remember his

---

52. Soelle, *Revolutionary Patience*, 7.

embarrassing perspective on the Peasant War.) If God is all-powerful as the term power is traditionally understood, then human beings can just sit around and wait on God to solve everything. Instead, Soelle wants us to comprehend God as power-in-relationship.[53] Soelle found this understanding of voluntary divine powerlessness and dependence liberating because it meant that God out of love chooses to share power with human beings. She says: "I sought to clear away understandings of God that, like dead branches, still hung everywhere in Christianity and from which I wanted to be free. I sensed very clearly that, as Teresa of Avila put it so well, God 'has no other hands but ours' with which to accomplish things . . . We need God but not the Mr. Fix-it who manages everything from above."[54] Soelle understood the only true power to be the power that empowers others. When God chose to become human in Jesus and thus share power with us, God demonstrated *authentic power*—the power of love which always respects mutuality.[55]

In Soelle's own theology, she loved to underscore the mutuality of God and human beings. She filled her writing and preaching with theological reversals that startle Christians who are steeped in traditional thought. Consider the following provocative examples: "The majority of Germans today no longer believe in God . . . I fear the stance is mutual. What reason could God have to believe in us?"[56] "God has to have friends or else God has no power."[57] And perhaps most mind-blowing: "God loves, protects, renews and saves us. One rarely hears that this process can be truly experienced only when such love . . . is mutual. That humans love, protect and save God sounds to most people like megalomania or even madness."[58] In all of these examples, we witness Soelle reworking and radicalizing the Lutheran tradition, establishing herself as a Lutheran liberation theologian of the cross.

---

53. Soelle, *Mystery of Death*, 81.

54. Soelle, *Against the Wind*, 32–33. Compare Bonhoeffer's rejection of God as a *deus ex machina*, as examined in chapter 3 above.

55. Søren Kierkegaard plays with similar understandings of a God whose power is the power of suffering love. See, for example, his "god poem" in *Philosophical Fragments*, KW 7:31, 55–56.

56. Soelle, *Against the Wind*, 95.

57. Soelle, *Mystery of Death*, 45.

58. Wind, *Mystic and Rebel*, 43.

The Power of Naming

As we have already established, a first characteristic of the theologian of the cross is that she discerns God's hiddenness and presence within suffering. Luther described a second characteristic: "A theology of glory calls evil good and good evil. A theology of the cross calls the thing what it actually is."[59] A theology of the cross calls things by their right names. Yet what can we reasonably expect will happen to the theologian of the cross when she or he calls things by their right names or calls a thing what it actually is? Luther suffered excommunication, arrest, a death-sentence, designation as an outlaw, and charges of heresy. Jesus warned of this exact outcome for those who speak truth to power: "Truly I tell you, no prophet is accepted in the prophet's hometown" (Luke 4:24).

Dorothee Soelle, as this chapter has unveiled, was a theologian of the cross par excellence. Not only did she discern God hidden in suffering and *sub contrario*, but she also spoke truth to power and suffered the weighty consequences. Interestingly, in Soelle's theological memoir, she gives a notable shout-out to Luther's thought for giving her the confidence to do so. Soelle explains that from Luther's translation of the Bible she learned a new word, *Freidigkeit*, a term Luther used to translate the Greek word *parrhesia* (which means boldness or openness, especially in speech) into German. *Freidigkeit* melds two words into one—freedom (*Freiheit*) and brazenness (*Frechheit*). *Freidigkeit* therefore means brazen confidence and free-minded speech; Soelle suggests that *Freidigkeit* should be the attitude of the true theologian.[60] In striking similarity to Luther's claim that a theologian of the cross calls things by their right names (but with her classic socio-political twist), Soelle writes: "Wherever one speaks of faith, the respective political and social conditions *must be named for what they are*."[61]

As we might expect given what happened to Luther, Soelle likewise discovered that being a practitioner of *theologia crucis* carried with it a heavy penalty. Soelle's uncanny prophetic ability to call things by their right names resulted in imprisonment, frequent arrest, denunciation by the Lutheran church, charges of heresy, and the inability to obtain a professorial position of theology in her home country of Germany. When people insisted that Soelle and the movements she was involved in were unsuccessful,

59. Luther, "Heidelberg Disputation," *BTW* 68 (thesis 21).

60. Soelle, *Against the Wind*, 23.

61. Wind, *Mystic and Rebel*, 134. Italics mine.

she would often answer with an incisive quotation from Martin Buber: "Success is not a name of God."[62] From her liberationist perspective, she suggests that "being arrested, criminalized, tried, and sentenced were important events in my life."[63]

Soelle was notorious for calling many things "evil" that most people within her culture—and indeed most people across the globe—called "good." For this reason, as Jesus accurately predicted, the powers-that-be rejected her. Soelle's children reported that throughout her life Soelle received "baskets full of hate letters."[64] Her biographer Renate Wind explains, "[Dorothee] was subjected to the fascist dregs of prejudice and hatred. Anonymous phone calls delivered threats and abuse; terms like communist pig were part and parcel of her daily life."[65] One Cardinal even labeled her poem "Credo" blasphemy.[66] In many ways, she joined Luther in becoming an "outlaw Christian."[67]

In particular, Soelle invoked ire because she dared to designate as evil the supreme inviolable good of Western culture: capitalism. In the last section of this essay, we will analyze Soelle's audacious attacks on this sacred institution in order to demonstrate how Soelle took Luther's idea of calling things by their right names to its radical limit, to places far beyond where Luther himself ever went or dreamed.

Soelle's Radical Prophetic Critique of Capitalism

Dorothee Soelle criticized capitalism as an inherently unjust system that necessitates the creation of social classes of winners and losers, rich and poor, labor and management, dominators and the dominated, owners and the dispossessed. In this regard, she was an obvious student of sociologist Karl Marx, who declared that capitalism creates class warfare and exploits the working class and oppresses them by prohibiting their ownership of the necessary means of production. Interestingly, Marx—a professed atheist—grew up in a Jewish-Lutheran home in a predominantly Lutheran society.

62. Soelle, *Essential Writings*, 73.

63. Soelle, *Against the Wind*, 119.

64. Wind, *Mystic and Rebel*, 160.

65. Ibid., 65.

66. Ibid.

67. See chapter 1 above. For more on this subject and for a clear definition of "outlaw Christianity," see Bussie, *Outlaw Christian*.

Soelle once made the following "jocoserious" comment on her relationship to Marxism:

> Later I often became impatient when Christian believers asked me, 'Are you a Marxist?' The best reply that came to mind was . . . 'Do you brush your teeth? I mean, now that the toothbrush has been invented?' How could you read Amos and Isaiah and not Karl Marx and Friedrich Engels? That would amount to being ungrateful to a God who sends prophets among us with the message that to know Yahweh means to do justice.[68]

Marx, though baptized as a Lutheran as a child, later became an atheist. He believed religion was an opiate that encouraged the working poor to accept the unjust socio-economic structures that impoverished them. In spite of Marx's atheism and condemnation of religion as a purveyor of the status quo, his thought deeply informed Christian liberation theology and adherents such as Soelle. Ironically, these theologians used the gospel and its religious principles to attack the economic status quo, thereby putting religion to a social use that Marx did not envision possible.

In Soelle's Christian adoption of Marxist views, she rebelled against reductionist, either/or cultural categories that demanded that Christians and communists/socialists be in opposition simply because of divergent attitudes regarding belief in God. Soelle claims: "The question of whether a Christian can be a socialist at all, that is, whether there is a socialism that lets go of atheism as one of its tenets . . . Today this question has become obsolete in view of the theology of liberation developed outside of Europe."[69] Intriguingly, Soelle credits fascism for liberation theology's birth, arguing that the place where radical Christians first encountered communists and learned from their ideas was in fascist prisons and concentration camps, where both suppressed groups shared "suffering and hope, cigarettes and news."[70]

Soelle found Marxist theory exceedingly useful for Christians seeking to follow a God who not only loved the poor, but loved them so much that (S)he became one of them through the incarnation. Christian-Marxist dialogue had such an influence on Soelle that it helped transform her theology into one of liberation: "The encounter with Marxism deepened my Christian understanding of the historical and social dimension of human

68. Soelle, *Against the Wind*, 47.
69. Ibid., 49.
70. Ibid.

existence . . . Hunger and unemployment, and the military-industrial complex and its impact on day-to-day life moved from the periphery to the forefront of my theological work."[71]

Soelle ultimately considered Marxist thought to be so compatible with the Christian gospel that she self-identified as a Christian Socialist. When asked why a Christian should be a socialist, Soelle replied, "Love your neighbor . . . The more you open yourself to your neighbor, the more you have to be concerned about the world your neighbor lives in; their housing, work and socialization, their overall life situation. The truly merciful person will in any case bite granite some day—that is, the structures of ownership and social class."[72] Of course, Martin Luther, who lived in the sixteenth century, did not have access to concepts or critiques such as Marxism or capitalism. Nonetheless, he laid a solid theoretical foundation for Soelle's ideas in his espousal of a strong, even selfless, neighbor-love ethic: "We do not help the neighbor as we are obligated to help him [sic], namely, with words, preaching, advice, constellation, and with money, goods, honor, body, and life . . . therefore we must all say to one another: 'I am obligated to you; you are obligated to me.' . . . We are not zealous enough, however, in seeking out people who need us and offering them our service."[73]

By listening to the neighbor, especially the neighbor in Latin America, a place to which Soelle frequently traveled, Soelle discovered that capitalism condemned two-thirds of the world's population to live in poverty.[74] Capitalism, in Soelle's understanding, was an economic system based on greed and exploitation rather than the sharing and cooperation that Jesus admonished. Such a system could not possibly be compatible with Jesus's instructions from the Sermon on the Mount: "Do not lay up for yourselves treasures on earth, where moth and rust consume . . . but store up for yourselves treasures in heaven . . . For where your treasure is, there your heart will be also" (Matt 6:19–21).

With regard to capitalism and its corollary injustices Soelle, as a public theologian of the cross, took a bold stand and scandalously called things by their right names. She often offended those in the middle and upper classes by distinguishing between an authentic Christian faith and what she termed a "bourgeois respectability." In a 1983 public address at the World Council

71. Ibid., 50.

72. Wind, *Mystic and Rebel*, 79.

73. Luther, "The Sacrament of the Body," 335.

74. For a moving account of her travels, see Soelle, *Stations of the Cross.*

of Churches, Soelle declared: "Between the impoverished and Christ, who signifies the fullness of life for all, exploitation intervenes as the sin of the rich as they try to destroy the promise of the abundance for all."[75] The price Soelle paid for this audacious speech was high—canceled programming by the BBC and other networks, condemnation from the German Protestant governing church body, and a revoked teaching invitation from a renowned youth institute. As both Soelle and Luther learned the hard way, a theology of glory does not countenance upheaval without retaliation.

Theologians of glory view some goods as so unambiguous and pure— or more accurately, as so necessary to their own power and privilege—that they seek to crush any critique of them. Soelle's unabashed *theologia crucis* stance of calling things by their proper names led even Ernst Kasemann, a liberal theologian who largely agreed with Soelle's views, to exclaim once in frustration: "Does she really have to go make a public statement on every injustice, mobilizing people to action everywhere she goes?"[76] By far the best summary of Soelle's position as a theologian of the cross who was engaged in prophetic culture-critique came from one of her Union Seminary colleagues who pronounced here to be "unrelenting when it came to exposing the injustice and greed of the Western Economic order."[77]

Yes, Soelle was undoubtedly radical in her sustained prophetic critique of capitalism. But, once again, she is radical only in the sense of returning to the roots. Wasn't Jesus outraged when he saw the money-changers in the temple, drove them out and said to them, "It is written, 'My house shall be called a house of prayer;' but you are making it a den of robbers" (Matt 21:12–13)? Even more importantly, didn't the disciples, those who knew Jesus and his teachings most intimately, decide to abolish private property and live a lifestyle that, in modern-day language, can only be described as communist? This lifestyle is relayed in Acts: "Now the whole group of those who believed were of one heart and soul, and no one claimed private ownership of any possessions, but everything they owned was held in common . . . As many as owned lands or houses sold them and brought the proceeds of what was sold . . . It was distributed to each as any had need" (Acts 4:32–34). Whenever I read Karl Marx, I am struck by the astonishing similarity between the passage in Acts describing Jesus's disciples and

75. Wind, *Mystic and Rebel*, 142.
76. Ibid., 67.
77. Ibid., 104.

Marx's own pithy summary of communism, "From each according to his ability, to each according to his need."[78]

Soelle argues for what she calls a liberation spirituality of sharing, and poignantly writes: "If we allow the dream that the hungry will be satisfied to be prohibited, then we have separated ourselves from God, or in any case from the God of the Bible. Capitalism does not forbid this dream . . . But sees to it that we forget the dream. When that does not work . . . the dream is made ridiculous."[79] I often wonder what Marx would think if he knew that in America today, the average CEO makes 380 times the salary of their own average worker.[80] If, as Bonhoeffer advises, you look at the world from below, from the perspective of the poor and have-nots, then communism sounds liberating and desirable. But if you are wealthy and one of the people (or corporations) who already *owns* the resources that others want to "share" and "redistribute," then communism sounds terrifying and world-reversing. Surely liberation theology sinks its teeth into a fundamental truth when it articulates as one of its primary tenets, *where we stand determines not only what we see, but what we want.*[81]

It is no coincidence that most Americans, who stand as a people among the wealthiest in the world, have been taught their whole lives that communism is the greatest evil on earth and that all of our resources must be used to combat its threat. But are we honest with ourselves when we ponder the real reasons why we have been taught that communism and socialism are pure evil and capitalism pure good? In her lifetime, Soelle was notorious for pointing out the hypocrisy in American (and Western) foreign policy. We are all for democracy, but not necessarily for democratically elected Central and South American socialist presidents who threaten to nationalize (read: socialize) certain natural resources such as oil and thereby not allow American corporations to privately own or access these resources. Against such presidents, we unashamedly fight wars in support of their brutal military dictator opponents—as long as those dictators commit to capitalism (think: Chile, Panama, Nicaragua, El Salvador). Soelle asserts:

78. Marx, *Critique of the Gotha Program.* Communism, which calls for the abolition of all private property, is more radical than socialism, which calls for only the means of production to be held in common. Soelle, who called herself a socialist rather than a communist, is therefore more radical than her capitalist counterparts but arguably not as radical as Jesus's disciples (or Marx).

79. Dorothee Soelle, *On Earth as in Heaven,* 64.

80. See Garofalo, "Average Fortune 500 CEO."

81. Brown, *Liberation Theology,* 36.

"That the capitalist way brings hunger, misery and increasing indebtedness for the peoples of the world . . . can no longer be denied. The democratic element that makes capitalism tolerable fails . . . The most barbaric military dictatorships were supported for decades by the superpowers when they guaranteed privileges, powers, markets, and tax advantages for capital."[82]

Certainly one must also consider the historic brutalities and human rights violations of socialist and communist regimes. We must not ignore such sobering facts. But we also must not focus exclusively on the very real failures and perversions of communism and socialism which have occurred in history, while completely ignoring the fact that today for the one billion people across the globe who live in abject poverty, capitalism has failed and become perverted in exactly the same way. For Soelle, this double standard in criticism is absurd and unacceptable. Instead, we must "try to hear the cry of the poor as God hears it."[83] Can we really say that capitalism is working in a world where my own shelves are ridiculously laden with Costco-size abundance, while 36,000 children die a day from starvation and simple infections? From Soelle's perspective, we cannot: "Capitalistic barbarism [asserts] that there are winners that there are losers . . . the winners have the right to live long and happy lives . . . And the losers? Well, the most important thing is to arm ourselves against them, or else they will all become terrorists. The real terrorist is the new totalitarian economic system under which we live."[84]

Soelle makes clear the connection she perceives between capitalism and the violent military industrial complex that scaffolds it. The private ownership of possessions means that we must arm ourselves to defend, protect, and keep those possessions. Capitalism, in Soelle's view, requires war and violence to sustain itself. She deems our quest for so-called "security" neurotic and all-encompassing.[85]

Capitalism's incessant reliance upon war led Soelle herself to espouse pacifism, a radical position Luther would have found unthinkable—in spite of the fact that, for the first 300 years after Jesus's death, Christians were pacifists who refused to fight in the Roman army. This difference notwithstanding, Soelle in her prophetic critiques against war and capitalism often found comfort, inspiration, and support in Luther's thought. Once during

---

82. Soelle, *On Earth as in Heaven*, 57–58.

83. Soelle, *Stations of the Cross*, 69, 112.

84. Pinnock, *Theology of Dorothee Soelle*, 26.

85. Soelle, *Against the Wind*, 116.

a protest against the military and its nuclear armaments, Soelle discovered that she finally understood Luther's old hymn, *A Mighty Fortress is our God*: "I also felt a kind of Protestant defiance, something of what Martin Luther expresses in his famous hymn, 'And were the world all Devils o'er and ready to devour us, we do not fear them all so sore, from God they cannot hold us.' . . . Suddenly it [the hymn] seemed to fit, because it was related to a life situation."[86]

Concluding Thoughts

If being part of a tradition means being part of both that tradition's continuity and its change, then Dorothee Soelle was a Lutheran through and through. The Lutheran tradition has long embraced paradox as the truth about faith and life. Soelle, herself a paradox to most Lutherans, embodied the tradition. She rejected Luther; she embraced Luther. She adapted Luther's thought; she adopted Luther's thought. She was a reformer of the faith, but she reformed through a radical return to that faith's original roots. In all of these ways, Dorothee Soelle was a Lutheran over, against, within, and beyond the Lutheran theological tradition. She was a radical Lutheran liberation theologian of the cross who captured the best of both her own theology and Martin Luther's when she proclaimed: "For something to be theologically relevant, it must 'awaken in us a new way of perceiving,' lift us out of the assurance of what we know, confront us with our own clichés, unmask us, change our relation to the world and, hence, our very selves."[87]

---

86. Ibid., 120.

87. Wind, *Mystic and Rebel*, 64.

For Further Reading:

Brown, Robert McAfee. *Liberation Theology: An Introductory Guide*. Louisville: Westminster John Knox, 1993.

Bussie, Jacqueline. *Outlaw Christian: Finding Authentic Faith by Breaking the Rules*. Nashville: Nelson, 2016.

Gutiérrez, Gustavo. *We Drink from Our Own Wells: The Spiritual Journey of a People*. Translated by Matthew J. O'Connell. 20th ann. ed. Maryknoll, NY: Orbis, 2003.

Soelle, Dorothee. *Against the Wind: Memoir of a Radical Christian*. Translated by Barbara and Martin Rumscheidt. Minneapolis: Fortress, 1999.

Wind, Renate. *Dorothee Soelle—Mystic and Rebel: The Biography*. Translated by Nancy Lukens and Martin Rumscheidt. Minneapolis: Fortress, 2012.

Discussion Questions

1. According to Bussie, Soelle extends—or radicalizes—Luther's dictum that God is found in the cross of Jesus to claim that God is found in any and every instance of human suffering, and especially suffering stemming from political injustice. Does this extension wholly revise Luther's insight? "Merely" extend it? Bring it to its logical conclusion? What?

2. What do you make of liberation theologians' idea that God has a preferential option for the poor and the oppressed? How does so-called political theology return to the biblical vision? How might liberation theology help one come to terms with recent grassroots political movements such as the Black Lives Matter movement?

3. How do you respond to Soelle's suggestion that God needs you as much as you need God? Do you find it offensive, refreshing, provocative, un-Christian, deeply Christian, or perhaps something else? What all is at stake in this suggestion?

4. Bussie ends her chapter by questioning the compatibility of Christian life with an unfettered free market economy, at least from the perspective of a Lutheran liberation theologian of the cross. Where do you find yourself agreeing with Soelle and Bussie here? Where do you find yourself pushing back?

5

You

Radicalizing Life's Calling

Jason A. Mahn

I was leading and teaching a group of fifteen students from Augustana College (Rock Island, Illinois) for six weeks in Holden Village, a Lutheran retreat center and intentional religious community nestled remotely in Washington's Cascade Mountains. Holden is a countercultural place. Long-term residents and short-term volunteers leave behind cell phones, internet access, automobiles, hair driers, and often hot showers in order to live and work in the Village. Unlike North America's dominant society, where labor-saving technologies and bureaucratic workflow diagrams reign supreme, people at Holden "waste" a good deal of time eating and talking with one another, knitting their own ski-caps, even earnestly debating—literally for hours—whether it is appropriate to listen to Christmas music in the season of Advent.[1]

People are drawn to Holden for various reasons. Some want to get "back to the land," to grow and prepare much of their own food, and to make their own music (guitars are plenty), pottery (there's a studio), or clothing (knitting is huge), thus bypassing their dependency on corporations and agribusiness. Others are drawn to the mountains and their beauty; they are out hiking, snowshoeing, or backcountry skiing whenever duties in the Village don't keep them inside. Still others are spiritual seekers—captivated

---

1. This last example is from Kaethe Schwehn's recollections of her year at Holden as a young adult: Schwehn, *Tailings*, 27–29, 34.

by daily vesper (evening) worship services, the labyrinth, or the laying on of hands and intercessory prayer that make up Friday's "prayer around the cross." Many are at transitional moments in their lives. College graduates in their twenties spend a "gap year" in Holden while applying to medical school or seminary. Widows and widowers find space and time to grieve. Retired Lutheran pastors meditate or journal again after decades of church leadership have left them spiritually depleted. Recent divorcees rediscover who they are—and who they are called to be—apart from the role of wife or husband.

We were about four weeks into our six week stint. I was teaching a class called "Creator, Creation, and Calling." As director of Augustana's Holden Term, I was also trying to check in with students and help address inevitable conflicts the best I could. One student—I'll call her Andrea—seemed distant, even avoiding eye contact with me. We finally found a few minutes to get a cup of coffee and figure out what was going on. Andrea named a number of ways that our coursework and other experience at Holden weren't living up to her expectations. The details are unimportant, except for this summary comment by Andrea, which I remember distinctly:

"I guess I thought Holden would be a more radical place."

What did Andrea expect? She had grown up visiting Catholic Worker urban houses of hospitality and agronomic communities founded by Dorothy Day and Peter Maurin, many of which publically protest war, corporate greed, and other structural evils. Did Andrea expect placards, megaphones, and sit-ins at Holden? Or maybe Andrea assumed that the manifest *churchiness* of Holden (evening prayer is mandatory) clearly counted as evidence against its radicalness. Can a community be liturgically, traditionally Christian and still be countercultural? Or are those mutually exclusive— the more churchy, the less revolutionary, and vice-versa? What would have even *counted* as radical? Can people baking their own bread or making their own entertainment or composting their own food waste count as such? How about those forgiving one another or debating whether jubilant Christmas music in early December detracts from the patience and hope that the practices of Advent are meant to help develop? Can extraordinary radicals be found engaged in very ordinary work—growing food, shoveling walkways, cleaning guest rooms, or teaching children? More to the point, *how* would that work need to be done in order to fundamentally resist the ways of our dominant culture, with all its emphasis on efficiency, disposability, individualism, and competitiveness?

Dietrich Bonhoeffer wrote that idealistic dreams about Christian communities—especially by newcomers to those communities—often lead to disillusionment.[2] People expect places like the Finkenwalde seminary[3] or Holden Village to be wholly different from our mundane, work-a-day lives and so lose hope in their "radicalness" when they discover that they, too, are filled with everyday compromises, conflict, and chores.[4] Truth be told, I was also disappointed that students on the 2016 Augustana Holden Term didn't get to see a typical—a "more radical"—Holden community, given that we were visiting while mine remediation workers were sharing the Village, complete with their diesel-burning generator, soda machine, imported surf-and-turf menu, and specially-streamed Super Bowl party. So the same questions above can be directed at me: What do I expect "radical" to look like? Will it always stand apart from the ordinary or conventional? Or can radical undertakings be found "in, with, and under"[5] the very every-day tasks of regular communities, colleges, churches, and their members?

This final chapter turns from well-known radical Lutherans/Lutheran radicals to people like you and me—people who probably think about justification and justice from time to time but who are daily concerned with paying bills, weeding the garden, writing term papers, or trying to be a decent spouse, parent, son, daughter, or friend. These daily tasks and responsibilities can seem worlds away from religious questions and quests—especially from the spiritual trials of Luther or Kierkegaard, the martyrdom of Bonhoeffer, or the unflinching political activism of Soelle. Yet Luther and the Lutheran tradition understand everyday work to be a primary response

2. Dietrich Bonhoeffer, *Life Together*, DBWE 5:34–36.

3. Recall that this was the underground seminary that Bonhoeffer led. In *Life Together* (written in 1938), Bonhoeffer reflects on life in Christian community in light of his experiences at Finkenwalde.

4. This point was brought home to me when visiting various Christian intentional communities as research for my book, *Becoming a Christian in Christendom*. One long-time member of the Rutbah House in Durham, North Carolina, complained that Duke Divinity students are all hot-and-bothered about living in intentional community until they figure out that this means helping to change diapers or washing the dinner dishes. In terms of everyday conflict, members of New Hope Catholic Worker Farm in Lamotte, Iowa note that what distinguishes intentional communities from other living situations is not the absence of conflict but the willingness to name it and deliberately work through it. See Mahn and Koleczek, "Intentional Christian Communities," 178–87.

5. The Lutheran understanding that Christ is really present "in, with, and under" the elements of a sacrament goes back to the Formula of Concord (1577), Article X, in Kolb, *The Book of Concord*.

to God's radical grace and the freedom it creates in a person. Indeed, they argue that God is at work in and through our mundane tasks and service no less than in a priest celebrating Mass or a pastor proclaiming God's Word. Luther called these jobs, tasks, and responsibilities *vocations*. From the Latin *vocare* (to call), or *vox* (voice), one *hears* one's vocation—or many vocations—by listening to God and for the neighbor in need.

Many assume that discerning one's vocation is an all-or-nothing quest to find God's plan for one's life—perhaps like Kierkegaard's single "idea for which I am willing to live and die."[6] Yet the tradition at its fullest and deepest has maintained that many vocations or callings can be heard "simply" by attending to one's relationships and commitments—to the people and places in one's life. I will here argue that such everyday vocations are just as radical—and just as indispensable—as the lives of history-makers, role models, religious leaders, and others we regard as "gifted." I will introduce a Lutheran understanding of vocation, raise concerns about the ways it has and can lose its radicalness, and then lift up one primary calling that each of us needs to hear and heed—the calling to care for the earth and its inhabitants.

Vocation Democratized

If you lived in sixteenth-century Europe and announced that you had a vocation or calling, it could mean only one thing—that you were (or were becoming) a nun, monk, or priest. These "religious" people, as they were also named, were alone *called* to work in service of God. Others—those who cooked, farmed, studied, cared for the young or the old, or had countless other jobs and tasks—may have done *needed* and even (in rare cases) *meaningful* work, but that work had little to no relation to God or the Christian life. Only "professional" Christians had vocations.

Luther was originally one of those "pros." As Samuel Torvend recounted in chapter 1, Luther surprised, and largely disappointed, his father when—still wet from the portentous thunderstorm—he announced his calling to become an Augustinian monk. Later, when Luther left the monastery to return to "the world," he took with him a new understanding of vocation. Any and every person was called by God to do God's work in the world. Luther's re-conception of vocation essentially democratized access to religious ways of life and even to eternal life, which was previously

6. *JP* 5:5100 (1835), p. 35. See Hughes's discussion in chapter 2 above.

thought attainable only by a select few. By proclaiming "the priesthood of all believers," Luther called all Christians to serve as "little Christs" to one another and thus to mediate the presence of God. [7] He also leveled the very distinction between what counts as "religious" and what was seen as "merely" mundane or "secular." Even today, changing dirty diapers or making a fair business deal do not seem like particularly Christian tasks. For Luther, that is because God only works though them as an actor works through a mask. The masks *disclose* God's presence, but also *hide* that presence.[8] Yet in referring to everyday, seemingly non-religious vocations as masks of God, Luther also asserts that God indeed is at work in and through the very ordinary undertakings of everyday people, even when we cannot see the divine directly. This lends credibility, or even sanctity, to what one normally considers the "secular" work of nurses, teachers, government officials, and so forth: "God wants us to honor and respect these 'positions' as [God's] masks or instruments through which [God] preserves and governs the world."[9] That God works through secular callings does not mean that they are unambiguously good, however. According to Luther, God can and does work through fallen individuals and structural evils, and they do not become less sinful in the process.

Behind this understanding of vocation is Luther's so-called doctrine of the two kingdoms. God works through both the heavenly and temporal realms, but accomplishes different goals through each. In the heavenly or right-hand kingdom, God works through the Word (meaning Christ as proclaimed in Scripture and in preaching) and through the sacraments to bring about justification and eternal life. In the secular or left-hand kingdom, God works through social, economic, and political structures[10] to continuously create and sustain the created world. In each, God works in similar ways: just as God's saving grace comes through the tangible means

7. To claim that all are priests should not underscore individual autonomy or an individual's unmediated contact with God, but rather the idea that any person can mediate God's presence to another. Luther is not an egalitarian in this and other ways. See Tranvik, *Martin Luther and the Called Life*, 113.

8. See Bussie's discussion of *deus absconditus*—the God who hides—in chapter 4 above.

9. Luther, "Lectures on Galatians" (1535), *LW* 26:96, as cited in Kleinhans, "Places of Responsibility," 106.

10. Luther described life as having three orders or arenas of activity—that of the household, the state, and the church. Many today would add paid work/professions to this list. See Tranvik, *Martin Luther and the Called Life*, 11–12.

of the sacraments (bread, wine, water), so too does God's preservation of order and care for the whole world come through tangible means–especially through the work of God's human creatures.[11] But while the means may be similar, the ends or goals of each kingdom (justification vs. creation and preservation) are different and ought not be confused. Thus, by distinguishing matters of salvation (the "alien" work of justification by God's right hand) from all other matters of worldly, although still Christian, concern (the preserving work of God's left hand, along with human judgment and effort), Luther not only expanded the language of vocation to include the 90 percent of the German population who didn't have callings into the priesthood or monastery; he also made virtually any worldly duty or office (*Stand*), paid or unpaid, compatible with the Christian faith. The irony should not go unnoticed: By clearly *dividing* matters of justification from any and every pursuit and ambition, "religious" or otherwise, Luther ends up with an *expansive* understanding of vocation. Almost any office or station in life thereby becomes christened, not because it directly contributes to the work of the Gospel but because it helps restrain evil, preserve order, and serve others.

These doctrinal details are less important than four main aspects of Lutheran understandings of vocation:

First, vocation as a theological concept is rooted in an understanding of God's *creation* and its preservation rather than in justification through Christ. Because they work to uphold the order and justice of the whole world, everyday offices and callings should be judged by how well they are done and whether they serve others, regardless of whether they are done in Jesus's name. Luther is thought to have said that a Christian shoemaker should not make shoes with little gold crosses on them but simply good, reliable shoes. Christians—in addition to Jews, Muslims, and many others—believe that God created (and still creates) the whole world and works to preserve its beauty, integrity, and orderliness. God calls all humans (and other creatures?) to partake in and preserve that creation. Vocations thus can be discerned and lived out by any person of good will—whether Christian, Jewish, Muslim, Buddhist, Hindu, or "none of the above."[12]

Second, discerning and living out one's vocation (or multiple vocations[13]) entails attention to the needs of others. Lutherans refer to these

---

11. Compare Kleinhans, "The Work of a Christian," 398.

12. See the Introduction above for a brief description of these "nones."

13. See Kleinhans, "Places of Responsibility," 99–121, as well as Mahn, "Conflict in

"others" as neighbors and to one's service to them as "neighbor love." Following the story of the good Samaritan (Luke 10:25–37), they mean by neighbor anyone who has hurts or needs to which another is capable of responding. (Luke's story of the good Samaritan even asserts that one learns proper neighbor-love from those typically scapegoated or demonized—in the biblical case, by a Samaritan, whom Jews held in contempt.) For Lutherans, then, it is less important *what* one does for work (paid or unpaid) than *how* one does it, and—most important of all—*for whom*.[14] The needs of the neighbor are decisive.

Third, and related, discerning what God is calling one to do entails attending to one's position in life and the relationships all around. Looking outward to others to discern one's calling would strike many as strange. If vocations are religious (that is, if it is *God* who calls), then we would think first to look upward or listen inward to see/hear our calling. On the contrary, Luther thought that the common roles we perform and the stations in which we find ourselves can help us discern our true callings:

> We have enough and more than enough to do in living aright . . .
> Just look only at the home and at the duties it alone imposes: parents and landlords must be obeyed; children and servants must be nourished, trained, ruled, and provided for in godly spirit. The rule of the home alone would give us enough to do, even if there were nothing else. Then the city, that is, the secular government, also gives us enough to do if we show ourselves really obedient, and conversely, if we are to judge, protect, and promote land and people.[15]

In a culture where being true to oneself seems the surest route to "authentic" discernment and choice, Lutherans emphasize the seemingly less dramatic work of reliably working through established roles and relationships. (Whether such established roles can lead to radical actions is a question to which I will return.)

Finally, the vocations of Christians should be lived out in a spirit of gratitude. As I have said, Lutherans assume that non-Christians also serve others and therefore have vocations and become the "masks" of God. Still, according to Luther, those who know Christ bring a distinctive ethos to

---

our Callings," 44–66.

14. Kaethe Schwehn, "Introduction," in Schwehn and Lagerquist, *Claiming our Callings*, 8.

15. Luther, "On the Councils and the Church," *LW* 41:177.

the responsibilities that follow God's grace. Without faith in God's gift, we might in fact "serve" for purely selfish reasons; Luther at least assumed that, without grace, we could not seek the welfare of others without keeping one eye open for the merit we were thereby accumulating. But once God's free gift of righteousness becomes "ours," we can and should "work with" it or help extend it as its natural "product," "fruit," and "consequence." Or again: "Then the soul no longer seeks to be righteous in and for itself, but it has Christ as its righteousness *and therefore seeks only the welfare of others*."[16] In other words, Luther believes that good work "should" be done not because one *must* do it or do it *in order* to get a reward but *because* God frees the Christian to serve others with genuine gratitude and care.

These four characteristics of vocation—it is rooted in creation, responsive to the neighbor, discerned by attending to routine roles and responsibilities, and marked by a spirit of gratitude—make calling a rather versatile theological concept. Lutheran colleges and universities, in particular, have found in *vocation* a way of naming the goal of church-related education. There was a time when a Lutheran college was a place where (mainly) Lutheran young adults went to be educated by (mainly) Lutheran faculty members and administrators. Those days are gone—and gladly so, for many of us. But what does it mean now to be a Lutheran college or university if it no longer means a place filled primarily by Lutherans? Answer: Lutheran colleges and universities are places where students from all religious and non-religious backgrounds learn to discern the real needs of neighbors and to responds to those needs with capable minds and grateful spirits for the benefit of the common good. In short, Lutheran colleges and universities educate for vocation.[17]

Certainly, this understanding of vocation is meaningful and versatile. Is it also radical? That is, can the understanding that God is at work through ordinary responsibilities and tasks, especially when they respond to the needs of neighbors, actually help forge solidarity with the poor and oppressed and other marginalized creatures? Can Lutheran understandings of being called go beyond interpersonal concern and care to help mobilize public protest against, and strategic reform of, systemic injustices? Does being called by God sometimes also call one *away* from dominant society, from its economic exploitation, cultural normativity, and nationalistic and

16. Luther, "Two Kinds of Righteousness," *LW* 31:299–300. Italics mine.

17. Kleinhans, "Places of Responsibility," 113; Christenson, *Gift and Task*, 24–31; Christenson, *Who Needs a Lutheran College*; and Wilhelm, "The Vocation Movement."

nativist appeals? We turn now to a number of keen criticisms of Lutheran understanding of vocation, many of which boil down to the critique that it is simply not radical—or Christian—enough.

Vocation Criticized

I have said that some of the largest proponents of Luther's understanding of vocation come from educators at Lutheran colleges and universities, who find in *vocation* a meaningful description of the very purpose of church-related education. While this is true, some of its most incisive critics come from those very quarters.

According to Kathryn Kleinhans, Distinguished Chair of Lutheran Heritage and Mission at Wartburg College, the difficulty with *vocation* comes from a dominant culture that so easily normalizes and domesticates it, imbuing work (and sometimes workaholism) with religious meaning and sanction. Especially in an age that focuses on personal fulfillment, it is easy to romanticize and trivialize "purposeful" and "meaningful" work. More dangerous still is the risk that affirmation of ordinary work may "devolve into a passive justification of the status quo or even an active cover for injustice."[18] When and how, asks Kleinhans, might doing one's duty with a sense of responsibility "become the 'just following orders' of Auschwitz or Abu Ghraib"?[19]

Similarly, Samuel Torvend recently pondered whether Lutheran "education for vocation" reinforces rather than resists the powerful cultural norms of individualism, narcissism, consumerism, "disposability rather than conservation," and careerism:

> I sometimes wonder if the vocation of a Lutheran college . . . has become the calling to serve as the unwitting accomplice in the acceptance of the status quo in which, ironically, we hope our students might discover their passion, their calling, their deep commitments.
>
> And if this is so, how easy it will be to snuff out and smother that first gift of Lutheran education—that capacity to ask deep troubling questions of what you and I, our disciplines, our

18. Kleinhans, "Work of a Christian," 397.
19. Ibid.

expertise, or our trustees might take for granted, consider normal, even sacrosanct.[20]

Marcia Bunge, the Bernhardson Distinguished Chair of Lutheran Studies at Gustavus Adolphus College, raised related cautions already in 2002:

> Because our culture glorifies individualism and self-fulfillment, speaking about vocation can also sometimes be a way of simply adding a spiritual gloss to a subjective sense of self-fulfillment. Here, one's vocation is what one does, whether paid or not, to find personal meaning and happiness. In this cultural context . . . there is little room for reflection on the relation of work to one's faith, to family life, to civic and environmental responsibilities, or to God's care and redemption of the world.[21]

In other words, invoking one's vocation threatens to become nothing more than "a convenient rubber stamp of approval on our lives or institutions."[22] To resist this temptation, Bunge suggest a number of strategies to Lutherans, including learning from Mennonite and other faith traditions that emphasize discipleship—the conviction that one's deepest calling is to follow Christ—as well as from the Catholic tradition, with its disciplines of meditation, spiritual direction, and other practices of "listen[ing] to the One who calls us."[23]

These "insider" critiques of Lutheran understandings of vocation boil down to a question of how those understandings *function*. Can hearing and living out one's vocation call one *away* from the status quo? When does it merely "rubber stamp" or give divine legitimacy to work that is actually self-serving? Or worse, when does vocation become the ideological justification of a power-grab by the privileged?

Similar questions have been raised by heirs of the Radical Reformation, that sixteenth-century reform movement that criticized Lutheran and Calvinistic reformers for remaing beholden to princes and other political powers even while criticizing the church's abuses. Radical reformers (also known as Anabaptists[24]) distinguished themselves from the mainline (or

20. Torvend, "Greed is an Unbelieving Scoundrel, 16.

21. Bunge, "Renewing a Sense of Vocation," 12.

22. Ibid., 16.

23. Ibid.

24. Literally, "re-baptizers." Radical reformers such as Menno Simmons (from which contemporary Mennonite Christians derive their name) rejected infant baptism because it served as initiation into both the church and the political state, thereby signaling

"magisterial") reform movement as early as 1526, when Martin Luther wrote "Whether Soldiers, Too, Can be Saved." There, Luther assured the prince's soldiers that when "being a soldier, going to war, stabbing and killing, [and even] robbing and burning" are required by military necessity, then Christians ought to do these things and not have a guilty conscience when they do.[25] According to Luther, it is only impersonal "offices" that wield the sword or pull the hangman's switch. The individuals fulfilling these roles can be fully Christian, just as capable of receiving salvation and doing good and needed work in the world. According to the radical reformers, such an understanding of vocation lends legitimacy and sanction to acts that directly contradict Jesus's injunction to love your enemies and pray for those who persecute you (Matt 5:44), and to forgive others up to seventy-seven times (Matt 18:21–22).

Like their sixteenth-century Radical Reformation predecessors, contemporary Mennonite and Amish Christians (all "Anabaptists") primarily critique Luther's and Lutherans' sanctioning of selective forms of legal violence (war).[26] As pacifists, they understand lethal violence (legal or illegal) to be incompatible with the central teachings of Jesus (especially his Sermon on the Mount—see Matt 5), as well as with Jesus's own willingness to die rather than kill.[27] More broadly, though, radical reformers and their contemporary heirs argue that Christians ought to restore the New Testament's usage of *vocation*, which means to call persons into a radically new and spirit-driven Christian community that is set apart from the dominant order. For them, the Lutheran (and other mainline or "magisterial") reformer's use of vocation, by contrast, functions only to "divine rubber stamp" the ways of the world.[28]

---

captivity to political power. The originally pejorative term "Anabaptist" accused them (often wrongly) of re-baptizing converts who had already been baptized as infants.

25. Luther, "Whether Soldiers, Too, Can be Saved," *LW* 46:95.

26. Luther alleviated the troubled consciences of soldiers soon after accusing peasant rebels (who held no official "office") of "cloaking" their own violence in the name of Christ. This can make him appear more than a little beholden to established political powers, if not altogether hypocritical. It was only *certain* consciences—those of persons acting with official governmental *authority*—that Luther was willing to comfort. He is least radical here, as Bussie indicated in chapter 4 above. Luther, "Against the Robbing," *LW* 46:50–51.

27. Recall from chapter 3 that Bonhoeffer was influenced by such Christian pacifism through the young French student Jean Lassere.

28. Yoder, *The Priestly Kingdom*, 210 n.9. Compare Hauerwas, "Work as Co-Creation," 48.

Roman Catholic liberation theologians likewise focus on how *vocation* sometimes functions to sanction the powers that be. This critique remains incredibly important, especially in prosperous, ostensibly "Christian" countries that so easily confuse being privileged with being blessed. Comparing mainline Western churches to the grassroots "base" religious communities in Latin America, the Roman Catholic political theologian Johann Baptist Metz finds that the church in prosperous countries

> has become here a form of bourgeois religion in which "Christian values" arch over a bourgeois identity without really affecting it in terms of a possible transformation or a promised fulfillment. Under the cloak of a merely believed-in (but not lived) faith . . . Christianity easily becomes the religious alibi for bourgeois innocence and the guarantee of a good conscience in a situation that really requires us to make the experience of guilt and failure in regard to these poor churches the very foundation of our everyday consciousness.[29]

I find these Anabaptist and liberationist critiques of standard Lutheran accounts of vocation exceedingly important, especially as we find it increasingly difficult to articulate the distinction between divine calling and personal fulfillment, economic privilege, or militaristic expedience. Yet, as the radical Lutherans featured in this book demonstrate, Lutherans can creatively rework their understandings of being called so that they do not simply justify and legitimize what might be unholy work. Bonhoeffer preferred to speak of "orders of preservation" and of "mandates" rather than created orders and eternal laws in order to emphasize that no vocation or office— no matter how officially sanctioned or seemingly necessary—should be occupied without asking troubling questions about how one should follow Christ from within it. Even when this self-proclaimed pacifist became involved in a conspiracy plot to kill Hitler, he refused to justify his or his co-conspirators' actions as "right," and much less as "Christian." By his estimation, they all were indefensibly sinful, fully thrown on the grace and forgiveness of God.[30] Kierkegaard says something similar when thinking through the depiction in Genesis 22 of Abraham's willingness to kill Isaac at the summoning of God. Abraham's actions remain unjustifiable, according

---

29. Metz, *The Emergent Church*, 76–77.

30. See Bonhoeffer, *Ethics*, DBWE 6:131, 274, and Hale's discussion in chapter 3 above. Bonhoeffer rejects "the justification and sanctification of the worldly orders as such" as "pseudo-Lutheran." Bonhoeffer, *Ethics*, DBWE 6:289, as cited in Kleinhans, "Places of Responsibility," 109.

to any moral or human accounting. One ought not to call them "necessary" or "ethical" or even "understandable," although they may very well be faithful.[31] Finally, while Soelle sometimes starkly contrasts political revolution (represented by Thomas Münster, a radical reformer), with the theological reformation (represented by Martin Luther),[32] she also finds the grounding of the first in the second, as Bussie has shown.

Are North American Christians capable of raising critical questions about their country's economies, politics, military strategies, and other central undertakings, distinguishing them from the calling of Christians to discipleship and stoking the consciences of those who feel pulled between each? Or does it primarily function as a "religious alibi," guarantee a good conscience, and otherwise put a "divine rubber stamp" on the ways of the world, thus allowing things to run all too smoothly?

To put it more personally, and in the second-person voice of this chapter's title: What about *your* sense of vocation, of being called? Does that calling often or always affirm projects and professions that you find fulfilling and rewarding, and for which you are rewarded? Or do you sometimes also feel called to do justice, love kindness, and walk humbly with God (see Micah 6:8)—even when those undertakings are inconvenient, unrewarded, monotonous, or even precarious? Are you always called *toward* meaningful and purposeful work? Are you ever called *away* from unjust and unsustainable work, even if that means accepting less status and security or looking naïve to the "ways of the world"?

Vocation Radicalized

Thus far in this chapter, I have (1) highlighted central characteristics of Lutheran understandings of vocation—including, its rootedness in creation, its responsiveness to neighbors in need, its attention to routine roles and responsibilities, and its being marked by a spirit of gratitude. I have also (2) repeated invaluable critiques of this understanding, from both inside and outside the Lutheran tradition, insofar as it tends to give divine sanction to work that may in fact be unjust or even unchristian. In the spirit of this entire book, which demonstrates how the deepest roots of the Lutheran tradition can bloom into socio-political resistance to the status quo (including

31. Kierkegaard, *Fear and Trembling*, KW 6:54–67.

32. Soelle, *Suffering*, 129–34. Compare Moltmann, "Reformation and Revolution," 163–90.

status-quo Lutheranism), I want now to show how the four characteristics of vocation as delineated above might be radicalized to answer these critiques and directly lead to justice.

As a sort of extended example, I will focus on one particular form of justice here, that of ecological or environmental justice. I do so not only because it connects rather well with Lutheran understandings of vocation, but also because environmental degradation and exploitation of the earth lie at the root of many other injustices today. Consider, for example the connection between racism and environmental degradation. As many investigating "environment racism"[33] have shown, a disproportionate degree of hazardous waste gets dumped near non-white communities in the United States. Internationally, ecologically-dangerous factories are regularly transferred to countries of the two-thirds world, while "transboundary dumping" remains a common—if well hidden—way of exporting waste and relocating incinerators to the Global South.[34] Or consider the relationship between sexism and environmental injustice. As ecofeminists have shown, the way humans view the non-human world often parallels the way human males have viewed human females—as "only" natural, capable of being dominated and exploited for the upward "progress" of humankind, especially *mankind*.[35] Finally, consider how the poor are disproportionately marginalized not only from economic and political power, but also from the power that comes from being connected to the earth. The urban poor live with little access to the green spaces that have proven vital to mental and physical health. Many others living in "urban wastelands" find natural foods (that is, *actual* food) unavailable. Even the shrinking middle class remains bound to an economic system that forces too many to choose between unsafe and unsustainable employment (coal mining, for example) and the long-term health of their families and communities.

Given these deep, systemic connections between ecological injustice and ongoing racial, gendered, and economic disparities, we will not enjoy equality and justice until we also reconsider and rework humanity's

---

33. Benjamin Chavez, an African American civil rights leader, coined this term in 1987 in his study, "Toxic Wastes and Race." Many trace the intersection of race and ecological injustice to the 1980s when the North Carolina state government selected the poor and overwhelmingly black Warren County as the site for a hazardous waste facility. See Moe-Lobeda, "Climate Justice," 23–24. See additional sources in Johnson, "Turn to the Heavens and the Earth," xl n.18.

34. Moe-Lobeda, "Climate Justice," 24.

35. See Ruether, *Sexism and God-Talk*, 72–92; and Ruether, *Gaia and God*, 173–201.

relationship with the natural world. How can Lutheran understandings of being called by God to work in the world help? I return now to the four characteristics of vocation explored above, keeping critiques of vocation close at hand.

Called to Creation

Recall that Lutherans typically house their understandings of vocation in God's creation and its preservation, rather than in Christology (understandings of Christ) or the doctrine of justification. Many critiques of Lutherans on vocation land on this very point. Without turning to Jesus's (nonviolent) life and death as a concrete pattern for Christian work, "Christian" accounts of legitimate work would seem to legitimate just about anything.

Yet this critique tends to assume that creation and God's work as creator and preserver is without distinctiveness until Jesus comes on the scene. It also tends to set up a conceptual dichotomy between God's creating work and God's saving work in ways that are unsupported by lived experience and the witness of Scripture. (Standard interpretations of Lutheran "two kingdoms" do not much help here.) In reality, to understand the Creator as Caller and creation as called already presents certain ways of life as holy (and sustainable) and others as sinful (that is, exploitative, wasteful, and desecrating of God's good creation).

Notice that the first vocation recounted in Scripture—the one given to Adam in the garden—is of a very particular sort. In Genesis, God calls Adam (from *adamah*, Hebrew for *soil*) to till and keep the garden (Gen 2: 15). According to some, that vocation remains the quintessential calling of us all.[36] Just as God creates and redeems by "making room" for the flourishing of creation, so too is humanity called to the hospitality of "welcoming and enabling the whole of creation to share in the peace and joy of the divine life."[37] Humans are thus called to be co-creators and caretakers of God's creation, or what we now call the natural world.[38] The calling is so specific that some have concluded that "to garden is to enter into our most authentic vocation."[39]

36. Wirzba, *Paradise of God*, 18–34.

37. Ibid., 21.

38. James J. Farrell, "Good Work and the Good Life: Vocation as What We Do," in Schwehn and Lagerquist, *Claiming Our Callings*, 38.

39. Wirzba, *Paradise of God*, 118.

Does this mean, for example, that agriculture or horticulture should be the only majors offered by church-related colleges? Of course not. It does mean that other fields of study, passions, professions, tasks, and responsibilities lose their "vocational" status to the degree that they are done merely for monetary payoff or personal satisfaction, regardless of their impact on the created world. Christians should be willing to say that work for a corporation that sacrifices a community's health and sustainable use of natural resources for short term profits is *not* a vocation, theologically understood. It might be a career or a job, but it is not a vocation.[40] God simply does not call one to work *against* God's ongoing creation and sustaining of the earth. Humans are rather called to work with God for the flourishing of all creatures, human and nonhuman, whether that be through architecture, medicine, engineering, education, child-rearing, political leadership, or countless other vocations.

While this shared creative and sustaining work can be clearly distinguished from "personal" salvation in terms of doctrine, in lived experience the work and salvation are intricately intertwined. Salvation, in fact, cannot be restricted to what Luther meant by justification—an individual's "rightness" before God based on God's unilateral love and acceptance. From the root word *salus* (health), *salvation* refers to the total wellbeing (both physical and spiritual) or shalom of creation and all its creatures. Early "gnostic" Christians who divided salvation from creation imagined salvation as involving a release *from* physical bodies and this created world, rather than the health and healing *of* them. They were condemned as heretics by the early church. For his part, Luther also wrote and preached largely to reverse the gnostic flight of Christians from the material world. He sought to ground us, as it were, in the earth that is created and loved by God. *Vocation* is but one way of naming the heart of this incarnational and creation-centric theology. Moreover, Luther's primary way of describing God's hands-on work (and humanity's work with this work) was through *kenosis* or self-withdrawal: Humans, like God, make room for others so that they, too, might enjoy fullness of life. It is a vision shared not only by ancient Israelites,[41] but also by the best of modern science.[42]

---

40. For profound musings on the difference, see Orr, *Earth in Mind*, 16–25. I thank Jason Peters for pointing me to Orr's work.

41. Wirzba, *Paradise of God*, 136–37; Moltmann, *God in Creation*, 86–93.

42. Polkinghorne, *The Work of Love.*

If anything, gnostic denials that the earth is home have become more ubiquitous and frantic since sixteenth-century Germany. Very few of us would explicitly disdain the earth, but our economic, educational, and political practices often suggest otherwise. Centralized capital through the rise of multinational corporations has led to the de-skilling of labor, making workers less valuable and more replaceable. This leads to loss of job-security and a disinvestment of workers from the means and materials of their work—not to mention its meaningfulness.

For their part, those who are college-educated are rewarded with "upward" mobility. No longer stuck in the towns and communities from which they came, graduates are now "free" to move in and out of larger cities, where many will have less bodily contact with the natural world. Some will relocate (or often: *be relocated*) so often that "home" becomes literally anywhere and essentially nowhere. Another name for mobility: rootlessness.

Politically speaking, our nation's decision to tightly control the movement of labor through immigration policy while deregulating the movement of capital has the effect of keeping consumers less and less informed about who produces the goods they consume and under what conditions. Very few of us now make anything that we wear, build anything that we live in, grow anything that we eat, or fix anything we use—or know by name and character the people who do. (The local food movement is the most important counterexample, and the importance of it should not be underestimated.) Ignorance leads to abuse, given the fact that, as Wendell Berry notes, it is easy to abuse that which one does not love, and fail to love that which one cannot know.[43]

Of course, it is common in Christian quarters to hear the charge that the world is too materialistic, or the plea that people should love the Creator rather than the stuff of creation. I think this is rather misleading. Given how quickly we replace what we buy (much of it made with *planned* obsolescence), it would seem that we are much more addicted to shopping—to looking for the *next* new thing—than we are addicted to the things themselves. Given also how easily we leave local neighborhoods and church communities on one piece of land for counterparts elsewhere, certainly the problem isn't holding too tightly to earth. Rather, we seem *not nearly attached enough* to the places and creatures of God's good creation. If only Christians were *more* concerned with the materials of creation. If only

43. Berry, *Life is a Miracle*, 129–42.

Christians imagined salvation as the restored health (*salus*) of the earth, rather than salvation *from* it.[44]

Who is My Neighbor?

The Gospel of Luke recounts perhaps the most famous story by Jesus told in the Bible (see Luke 10:25–37). It begins with a lawyer questioning Jesus about what he must do to inherit eternal life. Jesus confirms the answer as given in the Hebrew Bible ("You shall love the Lord your God with all your heart, and with all your soul, and with all your strength, and with all your mind; and your neighbor as yourself").[45] The lawyer, "wanting to justify himself," then asks: "And who is my neighbor?" Jesus responds with the famous story of the good Samaritan, an outsider or non-Jew who helps a wounded man when Jewish religious leaders would not. The story radicalizes the command to love neighbors as oneself in two ways. First, Jesus calls into question any lines that we might paint between "neighbors"—those whom we know and who deserve our responsible care—and strangers or even enemies, those who lie "outside." Samaritans were foreigners who were not regarded as "neighbors" to Jews; by using a foreigner as an example of neighborly love, Jesus recasts the question to ask whether *anyone* would ever *not* qualify as a neighbor. Second, in Jesus's story the Samaritan does not *receive* an extended form of neighbor love but *enacts* it on behalf of, and as an example for, those who otherwise might exclude him. Thus, the lawyer learns what model neighbor-love entails from the very person he otherwise might exclude as "other."

Luther and Lutherans underscore this calling to love and serve those outside their circle of concern, and to learn to do so from the outsider's care of them. Luther's favored definition of sin was to be "curved in upon oneself" (*incurvatus in se*). To be redeemed from this sin or otherwise healed/saved thus involves being turned inside-out—from self-pride or self-loathing to forgetting about oneself, having been set free to see and respond to the needs of others. Admittedly, Luther largely defined sin as an *individual* turned in upon himself or herself and the graceful response to

44. Berry, "Christianity and the Survival of Creation," 149–64; see also Wirzba, *The Paradise of God*, 48, 83, 129; and Peters, "Wendell Berry's Vindication of the Flesh," 317–32.

45. Luke 10:27, quoting Deut 6:4–5 and Lev 19:17–18.

justification as a broader moral concern for other *humans*.[46] Should non-human creatures now count as the recipients of one's love and care? Are they also neighbors?

Environmentalists debate whether nonhuman animals have "rights," and whether the valuation of nonhuman creation should be based on an anthropocentric vision (based on human need and benefit), an ecocentric vision (based on the integrity of the whole ecosystem), or a theocentric vision (based on God's own loving care for all creation). By understanding neighbor love as decidedly unconcerned with reciprocity (one cares for neighbors based on their need, not what one might get in return), Lutheran Christians are well-prepared to understand anthropocentric ethics as a kind of curving in upon ourselves writ large, another unjustifiable demarcation of one community of responsible care (*homo sapiens*) from the rest of God's creation. What is more, Luther's theology of the cross claims that those who are marginalized and suffer bear God's presence in a special way. If clean water can be polluted, if the earth's climate can be distressed, if any sentient being can suffer—indeed, if the whole creation can await redemption with the groans of labor pains, as Paul suggests (Rom 8:19–23)—then certainly that very vulnerable suffering qualifies nonhuman species as recipients of human care.

Finally, recall from the good Samaritan that we often come to learn the scope and shape of self-forgetting hospitality from those we think *we* are called to serve. Might not nature itself provide such an example of hospitality and service—even an example of Christ-like love? Topsoil, for example, is the site of death and resurrection, a matrix into which every living thing finally gives itself away and from which each new germ of creation springs forth—by growing from the soil, or eating what is grown. The life of the soil thus entails a mysterious process of profound hospitality which makes room for manifold creatures to flourish, and then, receives them again into itself as nutrients for the renewal of other life.[47] What we might dismiss as mere dirt is, in the words of Wendell Berry, "very Christlike in its passivity and beneficence, and in the penetrating energy that issues out of its peaceableness."[48] We might here learn how to care for nature by attending to its care for us.

46. See the discussion in chapter 4 above.

47. Wirzba, *The Paradise of God*, 21–22, 27–34. See also Berry, "Two Economies," 219–35.

48. Berry, *The Long-Legged House*, 204.

Knowing One's Place

To discern one's vocation, one need only to look around at the given stations in life or offices that, according to Luther, one finds oneself occupying. For him, answering a calling from God thus largely entails being a good parent if you have kids, or a good soldier if you are recruited, or a good farmer if that is your estate. Many today find this given socio-political order far too static to be of much use in the contemporary world. Young persons, for example, do not simply accept a future path determined by their upbringing; even first-generation college students are free (and rightly encouraged) to pursue medicine, law, the academy, or any number of other professions that connect with their gifts and passions.

Certainly, we should reject much of the static socio-economic worldview that undergirded Luther's sense of vocation. But there are also insights there that ought not to be discarded wholesale. I noted above that much of today's gnostic flight from the earth comes from the western world's rampant mobility. With hyper-mobility and the so-called freedom to "be anything you want to be" also comes deracinated forms of life where people belong literally nowhere. (Social media and other virtual "realities" tend to exacerbate our condition of rootlessness.) Can a person discern her calling if she is not rooted deeply enough or long enough in a particular place to discern what the common good entails therein?

There's a necessary connection, I think, between discerning one's vocation and knowing one's local place—one's neighborhood, watershed, environmental niche, and ecosystem. For without an understanding of the fragile interdependence of the whole—which is always localized in particular ways—how can one take into account the gifts that one has been given and the debt of responsibility and service that one has been freed to repay? We are called not only to careers and aspirations *of our choosing*, but also to families, churches, and neighborhoods—as well as to rivers, forests, and community gardens—*each of which makes claims on us.*

Of course, "knowing one's place" can sound like a mandate meant to humiliate. At best, it is merely humbling, and in a positive sense. Humility is etymologically connected to *humanity* and to *humus*, the organic component of soil that is formed through the decomposition of organisms. When humans learn proper humility by becoming servants of creation—above and beyond being "successful"—they begin to develop "the authentic, ennobling humility that comes with an honest sense of [their] place in the wider world."[49] Environmentalists might call this an ecological ethic. Aldo Leopold called it a land ethic.[50] Lutherans call it the second form of righteousness, one whereby a human animal "no longer seeks to be righteous in and for itself, but it has Christ as its righteousness *and therefore seeks only the welfare of others*."[51] Knowing who those others are (all creatures) and something of their interdependence (ecology) necessitates that humans take root in particular places long enough to know the place and their place within it.

Grace and Gratitude

Most of all, vocation should be radicalized for the care and protection of the earth by underscoring that which makes it possible and calls it into being— God's free gift of grace. Given Luther's conceptual distinctions between a heavenly kingdom (the site of grace and justification) and an earthly kingdom (the site of God's creation and preservation, as well as the cooperating work of human vocation), many have assumed that the two have little to do with one another. In reality, there is absolutely no understanding of, and no place for, responsible human work in the world without God's declaration of a person's justification by grace through faith, apart from any work on our part. Exactly because God "does not desire works, nor has [God] need of them,"[52] one is freed to direct that work toward a neighbor who needs it, rather than at a God one is trying to placate. At best, then, vocation becomes responsive to God's grace. Such responsiveness is indicated in language about vocation: we *answer* a call, we *find* a vocation; we don't make or invent them. By understanding all human work as a response to God's gracious gift, Lutherans believe that *work* gains the full freedom, originality, purposefulness, creativity, and joy that it deserves.

The point here is that when Christians join Jewish people (or secular humanists, engaged Buddhists, or undergrad idealists) in the healing the world (*tikkun olam*), they do so with a spirit of gratitude. God has already accomplished what humans can never secure—right relation with the One who creates and redeems them. Having been thus gifted—indeed, gifted in

49. Wirzba, *Paradise of God*, 117–18.
50. Leopold, "The Land Ethic."
51. Luther, "Two Kinds of Righteousness," *LW* 31:299–300. Italics mine.
52. Luther, "The Babylonian Captivity of the Church," *LW* 36:42.

every way—people are freed to work from those gifts and with a sense of freedom and gratefulness.

Of course, there are Christians who ostensibly accept God's grace, understand themselves to be saved, and even talk loudly about the doctrine of justification, but who do not put God's gifts to work for the benefit of the suffering world. As Carl Hughes has shown, Kierkegaard critiques "the Lutheran establishment" essentially for confusing *grace* with a *doctrine* of grace, *being gifted* with *being privileged*, and *being free* with *having license and latitude*. As Lori Hale has shown, Bonhoeffer calls such license and privilege "cheap grace," while "costly grace" is that calling from God to a life of radical discipleship in service to those who need it—whether scapegoated Jews, endangered species, or the fragile ecosystem itself.

When it comes to care for a planet in peril, we must put grace to work with a spirit of gratitude. Indeed, it is creation as a whole, and soil in particular, that are primary sites of God's grace, a grace that we cheapen when we take it as anything other than gift. In the words of Norman Wirzba:

> To live intimately and sympathetically with the earth is to see that we are surrounded and sustained by gifts on every side and to acknowledge that the only proper response to this unfathomable kindness is our own attention, care, and gratitude . . . Working with the earth and making oneself vulnerable to its mysterious ways is to understand in the fiber of one's bones the difficulty and the hard-fought character of life. Grace is not cheap, nor does life come easily . . . [And yet] we [often] deprive ourselves of an appreciation for the costliness of God's good gifts, if we see them as gifts at all.[53]

That Kierkegaard, Bonhoeffer, or Soelle—and Luther too—have critiqued cheap grace in similar ways shows just how theologically astute and politically engaged such observations are. That a leading Christian ecologist is making them here shows that a full-bodied environmental ethic can and should grow from the soil that has also nourished radical Lutherans/Lutheran radicals.

Much of our economy tries to maximize monetary profit without concern for the health of the land. We extract minerals, burn fossil fuels, and develop labor-saving technologies that deny our connections to the web of life and render our bodies useless. All of this reflects "a denial of grace since

---

53. Wirzba, *Paradise of God*, 72.

it is premised on the seizure and then manipulation of the gifts of God."[54] Alternatively, when you pattern your activity on the hospitality of God's creation—when you grow real food, visit farmer's markets, bike rather than drive, repair rather than replace machines you need, refuse to buy and then discard machines that you do not need—then you align yourself with the creative and saving work of God. Indeed, you participate in the profound mystery, the utter miracle, of life as utter gift. You and I are called to work with grace, and to do so by caring for creation out of gratitude to God and compassion for fellow creatures.

Concluding Thoughts

This book as a whole has lifted up a tradition of radical Lutherans/Lutheran radicals for critical investigation, appreciation, and maybe even inspiration. The Lutheran tradition is one that is always reforming (*semper reformanda*). Who knows where the next shoot from this sprawling root system might grow?

As a reforming tradition, Lutheranism remains willing to work through (rather than reject wholescale or protest from without) fallen worldly structures in order to help hasten God's justice and shalom for all creation. The student who expressed her disappointment in Holden Village for not being "radical enough" perhaps sensed just how painstakingly slow and monotonous such work can be. Certainly God calls the faithful *from* unfaithful ways of life, and many radicals find themselves at the margins of political, economic, or cultural power. But justice often requires one to work radically with (that is, deep from within) unjust systems and fragile ecosystems, even if this sometimes risks complicity and often feels less than fully prophetic. I have focused on environmental issues here, but structures in need of redemption include nation states, the church, the economy, and established political avenues, not to mention hospitals, social service organizations, colleges and universities, courts, established professions, NGOs, the EPA, and the local PTA. Lutherans trust that God can and does use fallen structures—what St. Paul called the powers and principalities of this world—for good. And yet there is still the risk that the measured resolve to use such structures for slow and systemic change will provide convenient cover for waiting when we should be acting, for accepting as inevitable what we should be resisting and rejecting as unjust, unneeded, and unchristian.

54. Ibid., 147.

When Martin Luther King Jr. was locked up in Birmingham jail for one of his many acts of strategic civil obedience, he wrote to his fellow church leaders, urging them to join in civil disobedience out of obedience to a God of justice. Many of them thought King's protests and pleas were just and needed, but also too early, too rash, and too radical. King essentially had to explain to them "why we can't wait," why Christian discipleship and justice in the United States require pushing hard against the sinful status quo of segregation and bigotry.[55]

Martin Luther King Jr. was named after the sixteenth-century reformer, Martin Luther. If the latter were transported from sixteenth-century Germany to twentieth-century America, would the "reformer," like the pastors to whom King was writing, have encouraged more caution, less civil disobedience, than the "radical" civil rights leader was calling for? Perhaps. But as this book has shown, there is an alternative and deeply Lutheran tradition that includes theological resources for courageous work in solidarity with the poor and oppressed and exploited. Radical Lutherans/Lutheran radicals respond to a gift and calling from God. They answer justification by God with their own work for the justice of all.

And what are you called to do with this one wild and precious life of yours?[56]

---

55. King., *Why We Can't Wait.*
56. The language is from Mary Oliver's poem, "The Summer Day."

For Further Reading

Kleinhans, Kathryn. "The Work of a Christian: Vocation in Lutheran Perspective," *Word & World* 25 (2005) 394–402.

Orr, Robert W. *Earth in Mind: On Education, Environment, and the Human Prospect.* 2nd ed. Washington, DC: Island Press, 2004.

Polkinghorne, John, ed. *The Work of Love: Creation as Kenosis* (Grand Rapids: Eerdmans, 2001).

Schwehn, Mark R., and Dorothy C. Bass, eds. *Leading Lives that Matter: What We Should Do and Who We Should Be.* Grand Rapids: Eerdmans, 2006.

Tranvik, Mark D. *Martin Luther and the Called Life.* Minneapolis: Fortress, 2016.

Wirzba, Norman. *The Paradise of God: Renewing Religion in an Ecological Age.* Oxford: Oxford University Press, 2003.

Discussion Questions

1. Is language about "being called" or about "vocation" used within Lutheran colleges or church communities that you know? If so, how is that language used? More importantly, how does vocation language *function* in helpful and/or unhelpful ways?

2. Which critiques of Lutheran understandings of vocation do you find most important? Why? How can or should the Lutheran tradition respond to these critiques?

3. Does Gnosticism—the denigration of the body/earth while extoling spirit/heaven—remain a temptation for Christians today? If so, how is it best resisted? In what ways does your own sense of vocation intersect with humanity's collective calling to serve and keep the earth?

4. Thinking back on this book as a whole, which radical Lutheran/Lutheran radical did you find most compelling, troubling, inspirational, or otherwise memorable? Which dimensions of the Lutheran tradition are most worth preserving? Which require radical reformation or abandoning altogether? What role do you play—or would you like to play—in a tradition that is always being reformed?

Bibliography

Altmann, Walter. *Luther and Liberation: A Latin American Perspective*. Minneapolis: Fortress, 1992.

"America's Changing Religious Landscape," Pew Research Center: Religion and Public Life, May 12, 2015. http://www.pewforum.org/2015/05/12/americas-changing-religious-landscape

Augustine, Saint. *Confessions*. Translated by Henry Chadwick. New York: Oxford University Press, 1991.

Bainton, Roland H. *Here I Stand: A Life of Martin Luther*. Nashville: Abingdon, 1978.

Bayer, Oswald. *Martin Luther's Theology: A Contemporary Interpretation*. Translated by Thomas H. Trapp. Grand Rapids: Eerdmans, 2008.

Bethge, Eberhard. *Dietrich Bonhoeffer: A Biography*. Edited by Victoria J. Barnett. Minneapolis: Fortress, 2000.

Bethge, Renate. *Dietrich Bonhoeffer: A Brief Life*. Minneapolis: Fortress, 2004.

Berry, Wendell. "Christianity and the Survival of Creation." *Cross Currents* 43.2 (1993) 149–64.

———. *Life is a Miracle: An Essay Against Modern Superstition*. New York: Counterpoint, 2000.

———. *The Long-Legged House*. New York: 1969. Reprint, Washington, DC: Shoemaker & Hoard, 2004.

———. "Two Economies." In *The Art of the Commonplace: The Agrarian Essays of Wendell Berry*. Edited by Norman Wirzba, 219–35. Washington, DC: Counterpoint, 2002.

Blake, John. "The Black Panthers are Back—and Never Really Went Away." CNN, Feb. 17, 2016. http://www.cnn.com/2016/02/16/us/black-panthers

Bonhoeffer, Dietrich. *The Cost of Discipleship*. Translated by R.H. Fuller. New York: Macmillan, 1963.

———. *Discipleship*. Translated by Barbara Green and Reinhard Krauss. *DBWE* 4. Minneapolis: Fortress, 2003.

———. *Ethics*. Translated by Reinhard Krauss, et al. *DBWE* 6. Minneapolis: Fortress, 2005.

———. *Letters and Papers from Prison*. Translated by Isabel Best, et. al. *DBWE* 8. Minneapolis: Fortress, 2009.

———. *Life Together. Prayerbook of the Bible*. Translated by Daniel W. Bloesch and James H. Burtness. *DBWE* 5. Minneapolis: Fortress, 1996.

Bonhoeffer: Pastor, Pacifist, Nazi Resister. Directed by Martin Doblmeier. 2003. Journey Films Production. 2004. DVD.

Brown, Robert McAfee. *Liberation Theology: An Introductory Guide.* Louisville: Westminster John Knox, 1993.

Buber, Martin. *I and Thou.* Mansfield Centre, CT: Martino, 2010.

Bunge, Marcia. "Renewing a Sense of Vocation at Lutheran Colleges and Universities: Insights from a Project at Valparaiso University." *Intersections* 14 (Summer 2002) 11–18. http://digitalcommons.augustana.edu/cgi/viewcontent.cgi?article=1260&context=intersections

Burton, Nelson, F. "The Life of Dietrich Bonhoeffer." In *The Cambridge Companion to Dietrich Bonhoeffer*, edited by John de Gruchy, 22–49. Cambridge Companions to Religion. Cambridge: Cambridge Uni-versity Press, 1999.

Bussie, Jacqueline. *Outlaw Christian: Finding Authentic Faith by Breaking the Rules.* Nashville: Nelson, 2016.

Butler, Judith. *Frames of War: When Is Life Grievable?* London: Verso, 2009.

Carroll, James. *Constantine's Sword: The Church and the Jews.* Boston: Houghton Mifflin, 2001.

Chasmar, Jessica. "Greg Allen, Black Texas Police Chief, Calls Black Lives Matters a 'Radical Hate Group.'" *The Washington Times*, July 11, 2016. http://www.washingtontimes.com/news/2016/jul/11/greg-allen-black-texas-police-chief-calls-black-li

Christenson, Tom. *The Gift and Task of Lutheran Higher Education.* Minneapolis: Augsburg Fortress, 2004.

———. *Who Needs a Lutheran College: Values, Vision, Vocation.* Minneapolis: Lutheran University Press, 2011.

Come before Winter. Directed by Kevin Ekvall. 2017. DVD.

"Criminal Justice Fact Sheet." NAACP. http://www.naacp.org/pages/criminal-justice-fact-sheet

Eller, Vernard. *Kierkegaard and Radical Discipleship: A New Perspective.* Princeton: Princeton University Press, 1968.

Forde, Gerhard. *Justification by Faith: A Matter of Death and Life.* 1982. Reprint, Mifflintown, PA: Sigler, 1990.

———. "Radical Lutheranism." *Lutheran Quarterly* 1 (1987) 1–16. http://www.lutheranquarterly.com/uploads/7/4/0/1/7401289/radical_lutheranism.pdf

Green, Clifford and Michael DeJonge. *The Bonhoeffer Reader.* Minneapolis: Fortress, 2013.

Hall, Douglas John. *The Cross in Our Context: Jesus and the Suffering of the World.* Minneapolis: Fortress, 2003.

Hughes, Carl S. *Kierkegaard and the Staging of Desire: Rhetoric and Performance in a Theology of Eros.* New York: Fordham University Press, 2014.

Garff, Joakim. *Søren Kierkegaard: A Biography.* Translated by Bruce H. Kirmmse. Princeton: Princeton University Press, 2005.

Garofalo, Pat. "Average Fortune 500 CEO Now Paid 380 Times as Much as the Average Worker." https://thinkprogress.org/average-fortune-500-ceo-now-paid-380-times-as-much-as-the-average-worker-a174c85d62db#.1xerfmewf

Gutiérrez, Gustavo. *We Drink from Our Own Wells: The Spiritual Journey of a People.* 20th Anniversary ed. Maryknoll, NY: Orbis, 2003.

Hauerwas, Stanley. "Work as Co-Creation: A Critique of a Remarkably Bad Idea." In *Co-Creation and Capitalism: John Paul II's Laborem Exercens*, edited by J. W. Houck and O. F. Williams. Lanham, MD: University Press of America, 1983.

Haynes, Stephen, and Lori Brandt Hale. *Bonhoeffer for Armchair Theologians.* Louisville: Westminster John Knox, 2009.

Johnson, Elizabeth A. "Turn to the Heavens and the Earth: Retrieval of the Cosmos in Theology." In *Turning to the Heavens and the Earth: Theological Reflections on a Cosmological Conversation*, edited by Julia Brunbaugh and Natalia Imperatori-Lee, xxix–xlvi. Collegeville, MN: Liturgical, 2016.

Kierkegaard, Søren. *Christian Discourses. The Crisis and a Crisis in the Life of an Actress*. Edited and translated by Howard V. Hong and Edna H. Hong. KW 17. Princeton: Princeton University Press, 1997.

———. *Concluding Unscientific Postscript to Philosophical Fragments*. 2 vols. Edited and translated by Howard V. Hong and Edna H. Hong. KW 12.1 and 12.2. Princeton: Princeton University Press, 1992.

———. *The Corsair Affair*. Edited and translated by Howard V. Hong and Edna H. Hong. KW 13. Princeton: Princeton University Press, 1982.

———. *Fear and Trembling. Repetition*. Edited and translated by Howard V. Hong and Edna H. Hong. KW 6. Princeton: Princeton University Press, 1983.

———. *For Self-Examination. Judge for Yourself!* Edited and translated by Howard V. Hong and Edna H. Hong. KW 21. Princeton: Princeton University Press, 1990.

———. *The Moment and Late Writings*. Edited and translated by Howard V. Hong and Edna H. Hong. KW 23. Princeton: Princeton University Press, 1998.

———. *Philosophical Fragments. Johannes Climacus*. Edited and translated by Howard V. Hong and Edna H. Hong. KW 7. Princeton: Princeton University Press, 1985.

———. *The Point of View: On my Work as an Author, The Point of View for my Work as an Author, Armed Neutrality*. Edited and translated by Howard V. Hong and Edna H. Hong. KW 12. Princeton: Princeton University Press, 1998.

———. *Practice in Christianity*. Edited and translated by Howard V. Hong and Edna H. Hong. KW 20. Princeton: Princeton University Press, 1991.

———. *Søren Kierkegaard's Journals and Papers*. Edited and translated by Howard V. Hong and Edna H. Hong, assisted by Gregor Malantschuk, 7 Volumes. Bloomington: Indiana University Press, 1967–1978.

———. *Upbuilding Discourses in Various Spirits*. Edited and translated by Howard V. Hong and Edna H. Hong. KW 15. Princeton: Princeton University Press, 1993.

———. *Without Authority*, Edited and translated by Howard V. Hong and Edna H. Hong. KW 18. Princeton: Princeton University Press, 1997.

———. *Works of Love: Some Christian Reflections in the Form of Discourses*. Edited and translated by Howard V. Hong and Edna H. Hong. KW 14. Princeton: Princeton University Press, 1995.

King, Martin Luther, Jr. *Why We Can't Wait*. Boston: Beacon, 1963.

Kirkpatrick, Matthew D. *Attacks on Christendom in a World Come of Age: Kierkegaard, Bonhoeffer, and the Question of "Religionless Christianity."* Princeton Theological Monograph Series 166. Eugene, OR: Pickwick Publications, 2011.

Kleinhans, Kathryn A. "Places of Responsibility: Educating for Multiple Callings in Multiple Communities." In *At This Time and in This Place: Vocation and Higher Education*, edited by David S. Cunningham, 99–121. Oxford: Oxford University Press, 2016.

———. "The Work of a Christian: Vocation in Lutheran Perspective." *Word & World* 25 (2005) 394–402. https://wordandworld.luthersem.edu/content/pdfs/25-4_Work_and_Witness/25-4_Kleinhans.pdf

Kolb, Robert, and Timothy Wengert, eds. *The Book of Concord: The Confessions of the Evangelical Lutheran Church*. Minneapolis: Fortress, 2000.

Leopold, Aldo. "The Land Ethic." Excerpted from Aldo Leopold, *A Sand County Almanac*. Oxford: Oxford University Press, 1949. www.waterculture.org/uploads/Leopold_ TheLandEthic.pdf.

Levinas, Emmanuel. *Totality and Infinity*. Translated by Alphonso Lingis. Pittsburgh: Duquesne University Press, 1969.

Lindberg, Carter and Paul Wee, eds. *The Forgotten Luther: Reclaiming the Social-Economic Dimensions of the Reformation*. Minneapolis: Lutheran University Press, 2016.

Lipka, Michael. "A Closer Look at America's Rapidly Growing Religious 'Nones.'" Pew Research Center, May 13, 2015. http://www.pewresearch.org/fact-tank/2015/05/13/ a-closer-look-at-americas-rapidly-growing-religious-nones

Lohse, Bernard. *Martin Luther's Theology: Its Historical and Systematic Development*. Translated by Roy Harrisville. Minneapolis: Fortress, 1999.

Luther, Martin. "Against the Robbing and Murdering Hordes of Peasants" (1525). In *LW* 46:45–55.

———. "The Babylonian Captivity of the Church, Part I" (1520). In *LW* 36:3–126.

———. "The Blessed Sacrament of the Holy and True Body of Christ, and the Brotherhoods" (1519). In *LW* 35:45–73.

———. "Confession Concerning Christ's Supper—From Part I" (1528). In *Martin Luther's Basic Theological Writings*, edited by Timothy F. Lull, 259–76. 2nd ed. Minneapolis: Fortress, 2005.

———. "The Freedom of a Christian" (1520). In *LW* 31:327–77.

———. "Heidelberg Disputation" (1518), In *LW* 31:35–70.

———. "Heidelberg Disputation" (1518). In *Martin Luther's Basic Theological Writings* (*BTW*), 2nd ed., edited by Timothy F. Lull, 47–61. Minneapolis: Fortress, 2005.

———. "Lectures on Galatians." In *LW* 26:1–461.

———. "Ninety-Five Theses" (1517). In *LW* 31:17–33.

———. "On the Councils and the Church." In *LW* 41:3–178.

———. "Ordinance of a Common Chest: Preface" (1523). In *LW* 45:159–76.

———. "Preface to the Complete Edition of Luther's Latin Writings" (1545). In *LW* 34:323–38.

———. "The Sacrament of the Body and Blood of Christ." In *Martin Luther's Basic Theological Writings*, edited by Timothy F. Lull, 314–40. Minneapolis: Fortress, 1989.

———. "Two Kinds of Righteousness." In *LW* 31:293–306.

———. "To the German Nobility of the Christian Nation Concerning Reform of the Christian Estate" (1520). In *LW* 44:115–217.

———. "To Philip Melanchthon, Wartburg, August 1, 1521." In *LW* 48:277–82.

———. "Trade and Usury." In *LW* 45:231–310.

———. "Whether Soldiers, Too, Can be Saved" (1526). In *LW* 46:87–137.

Luther. Directed by Eric Till. 2003. MGM. 2004. DVD.

Mahn, Jason A. *Becoming a Christian in Christendom: Radical Discipleship and the Way of the Cross in America's "Christian" Culture*. Minneapolis: Fortress, 2016.

———. "The Conflicts in Our Callings: The Anguish (and Joy) of Willing Several Things." In *Vocation Across the Academy: A New Vocabulary for Higher Education*, edited by David S. Cunningham, 44–66. Oxford: Oxford University Press, 2017.

Mahn, Jason A. and and Grace Koleczek. "What Intentional Christian Communities Can Teach the Church." *Word & World* 34 (2014) 178–87.

Marty, Martin. *Martin Luther: A Life*. New York: Viking/Penguin, 2004.

Marx, Karl. *Critique of the Gotha Program.* https://www.marxists.org/archive/marx/works/1875/gotha

———. "Theses on Feuerbach" (1845). www.marx2mao.com/M&E/TF45.html.

McGrath, Alister. *Christianity's Dangerous Idea: The Protestant Revolution—A History from the Sixteenth Century to the Twenty-First.* New York: HarperOne, 2007.

Metz, Johann Baptist. *The Emergent Church: The Future of Christianity in a Postbourgeois World.* Translated by Peter Mann. New York: Crossroads, 1981.

Moltmann, Jürgen. *The Crucified God: The Cross of Christ as the Foundation and Criticism of Christian Theology.* Translated by R. A. Wilson and John Bowden. Minneapolis: Fortress, 1993.

———. *God in Creation: A New Theology of Creation and the Spirit of God. The Gifford Lectures 1984–1985.* Minneapolis: Fortress, 1993.

———. "Reformation and Revolution." In *Martin Luther and the Modern Mind: Freedom, Conscience, Toleration, Rights,* edited by Manfred Hoffman, 163–90. Toronto Studies in Theology 22. Lewiston, NY: Mellen, 1985.

Moe-Lobeda, Cynthia D. "Climate Justice, Environmental Racism, and a Lutheran Moral Vision." *Intersections* 36 (Fall 2012) 22–27. http://digitalcommons.augustana.edu/cgi/viewcontent.cgi?article=1065&context=intersections

———. *Resisting Structural Evil: Love as Ecological-Economic Vocation.* Minneapolis: Fortress, 2013.

"'Nones' on the Rise." Pew Research Center: Religion and Public Life, October 9, 2012. http://www.pewforum.org/2012/10/09/nones-on-the-rise

Oliver, Mary. "The Summer Day." In *New and Selected Poems,* Vol. 1. Boston: Beacon, 1992.

Orr, David W. *Earth in Mind: On Education, Environment, and the Human Prospect.* Washington, DC: Island, 1994.

Peters, Jason. "Wendell Berry's Vindication of the Flesh." *Christianity and Literature* 56 (2007) 317–32.

Pinnock, Sarah K. *The Theology of Dorothee Soelle.* New York: Trinity, 2003.

Polkinghorne, John, ed. *The Work of Love: Creation as Kenosis.* Grand Rapids: Eerdmans, 2001.

Rieth, Ricardo. "Luther on Greed." In *Harvesting Martin Luther's Reflections on Theology, Ethics, and the Church,* edited by Timothy Wengert, 152–68. Grand Rapids: Eerdmans, 2004.

Rubenstein, Richard L. "Was Dietrich Bonhoeffer a Righteous Gentile?" *New English Review.* April 2011. http://www.newenglishreview.org/custpage.cfm/frm/86357/sec_id/86357

Ruether, Rosemary Radford. *Gaia and God: An Ecofeminist Theology of Earth Healing.* New York: HarperCollins, 1992.

———. *Sexism and God-Talk: Toward a Feminist Theology.* 10th Anniversary ed. Boston: Beacon, 1993.

Schlingenseipen, Ferdinand. *Dietrich Bonhoeffer 1906–1945: Martyr, Thinker, Man of Resistance.* Translated by Isabel Best. New York: Bloomsbury T&T Clark, 2009.

Schwehn, Kaethe. *Tailings: A Memoir.* Eugene, OR: Cascade Books, 2014.

Schwehn, Kaethe, and L. DeAne Lagerquist, eds. *Claiming Our Callings: Toward a New Understanding of Vocation in the Liberal Arts.* Oxford: Oxford University Press, 2014.

Schwehn, Mark R., and Dorothy C. Bass, eds. *Leading Lives that Matter: What We Should Do and Who We Should Be.* Grand Rapids: Eerdmans, 2006.

Bibliography

Soelle, Dorothee. *Against the Wind: Memoir of a Radical Christian*. Translated by Barbara and Martin Rumscheidt. Minneapolis: Fortress, 1999.

———. *Dorothee Soelle: Essential Writings*. Edited by Dianne L. Oliver. Modern Spiritual Masters Series. Maryknoll, NY: Orbis, 2006.

———. *Mystery of Death*. Translated by Nancy Lukens-Rumscheidt and Martin Lukens-Rumscheidt. Minneapolis: Fortress, 2007.

———. *On Earth as in Heaven: A Liberation Spirituality of Sharing*. Translated by Mark Batko. Louisville: Westminster John Knox, 1993.

———. *Revolutionary Patience*. Translated by Rita and Robert Kimber. Maryknoll, NY: Orbis, 1997.

———. *The Silent Cry: Mysticism and Resistance*. Translated by Barbara Rumscheidt and Martin Rumscheidt. Minneapolis: Fortress, 2001.

———. *Stations of the Cross: A Latin American Pilgrimage*. Translated by Joyce Irwin. Minneapolis: Fortress, 1993.

———. *Suffering*. Translated by Everett R. Kalin. Philadelphia: Fortress, 1975.

———. *Theology for Skeptics: Reflections on God*. Translated by Joyce L. Irwin. Minneapolis: Fortress, 1995.

Solberg, Mary. *Compelling Knowledge: A Feminist Proposal for an Epistemology of the Cross*. Albany: SUNY Press, 1997.

Soulen, R. Kendall. *The God of Israel and Christian Theology*. Minneapolis: Fortress, 1996.

Stjerna, Kirsi. *Women and the Reformation*. Malden, MA: Blackwell, 2009.

Taylor, Charles. *Varieties of Religion Today: William James Revisited*. Institute for Human Sciences Vienna Lecture Series. Cambridge: Harvard University Press, 2002.

Torvend, Samuel. "Greed is an Unbelieving Scoundrel: The Common Good as Commitment to Social Justice." *Intersections* 42 (Fall 2015) 11–17. http://digitalcommons. augustana.edu/cgi/viewcontent.cgi?article=1192&context=intersections

———. *Luther and The Hungry Poor: Gathered Fragments*. Minneapolis: Fortress, 2008. Reprint, Eugene, OR: Wipf & Stock, 2017.

Tranvik, Mark D. *Martin Luther and the Called Life*. Minneapolis: Fortress, 2016.

Wallis, Jim. *America's Original Sin: Racism, White Privilege, and the Bridge to a New America*. Grand Rapids: Brazos, 2016.

Wiesel, Elie. *Night*. Translated by Stella Rodway. New York: Bantam, 1960.

Wiesenthal, Simon. *The Sunflower: On the Possibilities and Limits of Forgiveness*. New York: Schocken, 1997.

Wilhelm, Mark. "The Vocation Movement in Lutheran Higher Education." *Intersections* 43 (Spring 2016) 14–18. http://digitalcommons.augustana.edu/cgi/viewcontent.cgi?article=1395&context=intersections

Wind, Renate. *Dorothee Soelle—Mystic and Rebel: The Biography*. Translated by Nancy Lukens and Martin Rumscheidt. Minneapolis: Fortress, 2012.

Wirzba, Norman. *The Paradise of God: Renewing Religion in an Ecological Age*. Oxford: Oxford University Press, 2003.

Wyschogrod, Michael. *Abraham's Promise: Judaism and Jewish-Christian Relations*. Edited by R. Kendall Soulen. Grand Rapids: Eerdmans, 2004.

Yoder, John Howard. *The Priestly Kingdom: Social Ethics as Gospel*. South Bend, IN: University of Notre Dame Press, 2008.

Index